jQuery Game Development Essentials

Learn how to make fun and addictive multi-platform games using jQuery

Selim Arsever

PUBLISHING

BIRMINGHAM - MUMBAI

jQuery Game Development Essentials

First published: April 2013

Production Reference: 1180413

Published by Packt Publishing Ltd.
Livery Place
35 Livery Street
Birmingham B3 2PB, UK.

ISBN 978-1-84969-506-0

www.packtpub.com

Cover Image by Selim Arsever (selim.arsever@gmail.com)

Credits

Author

Selim Arsever

Reviewers

Samuel Lee Deering

Acquisition Editors

Erol Staveley

Edward Gordon

Lead Technical Editor

Ankita Shashi

Technical Editors

Kirti Pujari

Lubna Shaikh

Copy Editors

Brandt D'Mello

Insiya Morbiwala

Alfida Paiva

Laxmi Subramanian

Project Coordinator

Anugya Khurana

Proofreader

Maria Gould

Indexer

Hemangini Bari

Graphics

Sheetal Aute

Production Coordinator

Aparna Bhagat

Cover Work

Aparna Bhagat

About the Author

Selim Arsever is a Senior Software Engineer working as a consultant in Switzerland. Over the last 4 years, he has been developing gameQuery (`http://gamequeryjs.com`), an open source game engine based on jQuery, as well as other JavaScript games and demos. He has been giving several talks on the subject and thinks that there is nothing more interesting than using tools beyond what they were initially intended for. You can follow him on twitter at `@SelimArsever`.

Thank you to my wife and my son for their patience and support, and to the entire JavaScript community for their passion and openness.

About the Reviewer

Samuel Lee Deering is a Web Developer from England who specializes in JavaScript and jQuery. Sam has built his expertise from a strong programming background, including a Bachelor's degree in Computer Science, and has worked for several high-profile companies such as Flight Centre. Sam has a very strong web presence; he develops modern web apps and has written online publications for renowned websites, such as jQuery Mobile Builder and Smashing Magazine. Sam's main focus is to help improve the Web, and he shares his knowledge with millions on his blog at `http://www.jquery4u.com/`.

You can find his details on the following websites:

- **Profile picture**: `http://gravatar.com/samdeering`
- **Website**: `http://samdeering.com`
- **Blog**: `http://jquery4u.com`
- **Twitter**: `@samdeering @jquery4u`

www.PacktPub.com

Support files, eBooks, discount offers and more

You might want to visit www.PacktPub.com for support files and downloads related to your book.

Did you know that Packt offers eBook versions of every book published, with PDF and ePub files available? You can upgrade to the eBook version at www.PacktPub.com and as a print book customer, you are entitled to a discount on the eBook copy. Get in touch with us at service@packtpub.com for more details.

At www.PacktPub.com, you can also read a collection of free technical articles, sign up for a range of free newsletters and receive exclusive discounts and offers on Packt books and eBooks.

http://PacktLib.PacktPub.com

Do you need instant solutions to your IT questions? PacktLib is Packt's online digital book library. Here, you can access, read and search across Packt's entire library of books.

Why Subscribe?

- Fully searchable across every book published by Packt
- Copy and paste, print and bookmark content
- On demand and accessible via web browser

Free Access for Packt account holders

If you have an account with Packt at www.PacktPub.com, you can use this to access PacktLib today and view nine entirely free books. Simply use your login credentials for immediate access.

Table of Contents

Preface

Writing games is not only fun but also a very good way to learn a technology through and through. Even though HTML and JavaScript weren't conceived to run games, over the last few years, a series of events have occurred to make writing games in JavaScript a viable solution:

- Performance of browsers' JavaScript engines has improved dramatically, with modern engines being ten times faster than the state of the art engines in 2008
- jQuery and other similar libraries made working with the DOM as painless as it can be
- Flash lost a lot of ground due, in part, to its absence on iOS
- W3C started work on many game-oriented APIs such as canvas, WebGL, and full-screen APIs

Throughout this book, you will make three games and learn a wide array of techniques. You will not only be able to use your own games, but most importantly you will have fun doing so!

What this book covers

Chapter 1, jQuery for Games, provides an in-depth look at jQuery's functions that might be useful for game development.

Chapter 2, Creating Our First Game, implements a simple game with sprites, animation, and preloading.

Chapter 3, Better, Faster, but not Harder, optimizes the game we saw in *Chapter 2, Creating Our First Game*, with various techniques such as time-out inlining, keyboard polling, and HTML fragments.

Chapter 4, Looking Sideways, codes a platformer game with tile maps and collision detection.

Chapter 5, Putting Things into Perspective, creates an orthogonal RPG with tile map optimization, sprite occlusion, and better collision detection.

Chapter 6, Adding Levels to Your Games, expands the game we saw in *Chapter 4, Looking Sideways*, by adding multiple levels using JSON and AJAX.

Chapter 7, Making a Multiplayer Game, transforms the games we saw in *Chapter 5, Putting Things into Perspective*, to support multiple players on multiple machines.

Chapter 8, Let's Get Social, integrates the platform game with Facebook and Twitter as well as creating a cheat-proof leaderboard.

Chapter 9, Making Your Game Mobile, optimizes the games we saw in *Chapter 5, Putting Things into Perspective*, for mobile devices and touch control.

Chapter 10, Making Some Noise, adds sound effects and music to your game with the audio element, the Web Audio API, or Flash.

What you need for this book

One of the advantages of working with web technologies is that you won't need any complex or costly software to get you started. For strictly client-side games, you will only need your favorite code editor (or even a simple text editor, if you don't mind working without any syntax highlighting). If you haven't chosen any yet, there is plenty of free software around you that you could try, ranging from very old-school, such as VIM (http://www.vim.org/) and Emacs (http://www.gnu.org/software/emacs/) to more modern, such as Eclipse (http://www.eclipse.org/) and Aptana (http://www.aptana.com/), Notepad++ (http://notepad-plus-plus.org/), or Komodo Edit (http://www.activestate.com/komodo-edit). These are only some of the available editors that you can find. For JavaScript, you don't need a very advanced editor, so just use the one you're more familiar with.

If you create you own graphic, you will also need an image editing software. Here again, you will have a lot of choice. The most famous open source software being Gimp (http://www.gimp.org/) and one of my personal favorites, Pixen (http://pixenapp.com/).

For the part of the book that needs some server-side scripts, we will use PHP and MySQL. If you don't already have a server that supports them, to install these on your machine, you can use MAMP (http://www.mamp.info/), XAMPP (http://www.apachefriends.org/en/xampp.html), or EasyPHP (http://www.easyphp.org/) depending upon your OS.

Who this book is for

The primary audience for this book is a beginner web developer with some experience in JavaScript and jQuery. Since the server-side part is implemented in PHP, it will help if you have some knowledge of it too, but if you're more comfortable with another server-side language, you could use it instead of PHP without too much trouble.

You won't need any prior knowledge of game development at all to enjoy this book!

Conventions

In this book, you will find a number of styles of text that distinguish between different kinds of information. Here are some examples of these styles, and an explanation of their meaning.

Code words in text are shown as follows: "The .animate() function from jQuery allows you to make a property vary through time from the current value to a new one."

A block of code is set as follows:

```
$("#myElementId")
.animate({top: 200})
.animate({left: 200})
.dequeue();
```

When we wish to draw your attention to a particular part of a code block, the relevant lines or items are set in bold:

```
gf.keyboard = [];
// keyboard state handler
 $(document).keydown(function(event){
     gf.keyboard[event.keyCode] = true;
});
$(document).keyup(function(event){
     gf.keyboard[event.keyCode] = false;
});
```

Any command-line input or output is written as follows:

```
# cp /usr/src/asterisk-addons/configs/cdr_mysql.conf.sample
    /etc/asterisk/cdr_mysql.conf
```

New terms and **important words** are shown in bold. Words that you see on the screen, in menus or dialog boxes for example, appear in the text like this: "The following figure shows what a typical one-dimensional intersection **i** of two segments **a** and **b** would look like".

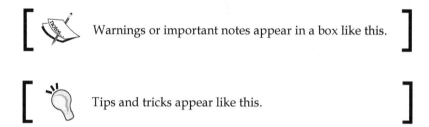

[Warnings or important notes appear in a box like this.]

[Tips and tricks appear like this.]

Reader feedback

Feedback from our readers is always welcome. Let us know what you think about this book—what you liked or may have disliked. Reader feedback is important for us to develop titles that you really get the most out of.

To send us general feedback, simply send an e-mail to feedback@packtpub.com, and mention the book title via the subject of your message.

If there is a topic that you have expertise in and you are interested in either writing or contributing to a book, see our author guide on www.packtpub.com/authors.

Customer support

Now that you are the proud owner of a Packt book, we have a number of things to help you to get the most from your purchase.

Downloading the example code

You can download the example code files for all Packt books you have purchased from your account at http://www.packtpub.com. If you purchased this book elsewhere, you can visit http://www.packtpub.com/support and register to have the files e-mailed directly to you.

Errata

Although we have taken every care to ensure the accuracy of our content, mistakes do happen. If you find a mistake in one of our books—maybe a mistake in the text or the code—we would be grateful if you would report this to us. By doing so, you can save other readers from frustration and help us improve subsequent versions of this book. If you find any errata, please report them by visiting http://www.packtpub.com/submit-errata, selecting your book, clicking on the **errata submission form** link, and entering the details of your errata. Once your errata are verified, your submission will be accepted and the errata will be uploaded on our website, or added to any list of existing errata, under the Errata section of that title. Any existing errata can be viewed by selecting your title from http://www.packtpub.com/support.

Piracy

Piracy of copyright material on the Internet is an ongoing problem across all media. At Packt, we take the protection of our copyright and licenses very seriously. If you come across any illegal copies of our works, in any form, on the Internet, please provide us with the location address or website name immediately so that we can pursue a remedy.

Please contact us at copyright@packtpub.com with a link to the suspected pirated material.

We appreciate your help in protecting our authors, and our ability to bring you valuable content.

Questions

You can contact us at questions@packtpub.com if you are having a problem with any aspect of the book, and we will do our best to address it.

1
jQuery for Games

Over the course of the last few years, jQuery has almost become the default framework for any JavaScript development. More than 55 percent of the top 10,000 most visited websites as well as an estimated total of 24 million websites on the Internet are using it (more at `http://trends.builtwith.com/javascript/JQuery`). And this trend doesn't show any sign of stopping.

This book expects you to have some prior experience of jQuery. If you feel that you don't meet this requirement, then you could first learn more about it in *Learning jQuery, Jonathan Chaffer, Karl Swedberg, Packt Publishing*.

This chapter will quickly go through the peculiarities of jQuery and will then dive deeper into its most game-oriented functions. Even if you probably have already used most of them, you may not be familiar with the full extent of their capabilities. The following is a detailed list of the topics addressed in this chapter:

- The peculiarities of jQuery
- The function that will help you for moving elements around
- Event handling
- DOM manipulation

The way of jQuery

jQuery's philosophy differs from most other JavaScript frameworks that predated it. Understanding the design patterns it uses is key to writing readable and efficient code. We'll cover these patterns in the next sections.

Chaining

Most jQuery statements are of the following form: a selection followed by one or more actions. The way those actions are combined is called chaining and is one of the most elegant aspects of jQuery. A beginner using jQuery who wants to set the width of an element to 300 pixels and its height to 100 pixels would typically write something like:

```
$("#myElementId").width(300);
$("#myElementId").height(100);
```

With chaining, this would be written as:

```
$("#myElementId").width(300).height(100);
```

This has many advantages: the element is selected only once, and the resulting code is more compact and conveys the semantic meaning that what you want to achieve is really only one thing, which is to change the element size.

Functions that allow chaining don't only make it possible to group many calls on the same object, but also there are many ways to actually change on what object (or objects) the next function on the chain will operate. In these situations, it is typical to use indentation to convey the idea that you're not working on the same elements as the previous indentation level.

For example, the following chain first selects an element, then sets its background's color as red. It then changes the elements in the chain to the children of the previous element and changes their background-color attribute to yellow.

```
$("#myElementId").css("background-color", "red")
    .children().css("background-color", "yellow");
```

It's important that you always ask yourself how the current interactions with the previous and next element in the chain can be avoided for undesired behavior.

Polymorphism

jQuery has its own way to use polymorphism, and a given function can be called in a lot of different ways depending on how much information you want to give to it. Let's have a look at the .css() function. If called with a String data type as the only argument, this function will behave as a getter by returning the value of the CSS property you asked for.

For example, the following line retrieves the left-hand side position of a given element (assuming it's positioned absolutely):

```
var elementLeft = $("#myElementId").css("left");
```

However, if you pass a second argument, it will start to behave like a setter and set the value of the CSS property. The interesting thing is that the second argument can also be a function. In this situation, the function is expected to return the value that will be set to the CSS property.

The following code does just that and uses a function that will increase the left-hand side position of the element by one:

```
$("#myElementId").css("left", function(index, value){
    return parseInt(value)+1;
});
```

However; wait, there's more! If you pass just one element to the same function, but that element is an object literal, then it will be considered as holding a map of properties/values. This will allow you to change many CSS properties in one single call, like setting the left and top position to 100 pixels in the following example:

```
$("#myElementId").css({
    left: 100,
    top: 100
});
```

You can also use strings as the key and value of your object literal as it's done in JSON.

A very complete resource for finding about all the ways to call a function is the jQuery API website (`http://api.jquery.com`).

We will now focus on a few functions that are of interest for developing games.

Moving things around

Chaining has a slightly different signification for animation. Though you may never actually need to use jQuery animation functions in most of your games, it may still be interesting to see the peculiarities of their functioning as it may be the cause of many strange behaviors.

Chaining animations

The `.animate()` function from jQuery allows you to make a property vary through time from the current value to a new one. A typical effect, for example, would be to move it left from 10 pixels, or change its height. From what you've seen earlier and experienced for other type of functions, you may expect the following code to make a div (DOM division element) move diagonally to the position `left` = 200px and `top` = 200px.

```
$("#myElementId").animate({top: 200}).animate({left: 200});
```

However, it doesn't! What you will see instead is the div first moves to reach `top` = 200px and only then moves to `left` = 200px. This is called queuing; each call to `animate` will be queued to the previous ones and will only execute once they're all finished. If you want to have two movements executed at the same time, thereby generating a diagonal movement, you'll have to use only one call to `.animate()`.

```
$("#myElementId").animate({top: 200,left: 200});
```

Another possibility is to explicitly tell the `.animate()` function not to queue the animations:

```
$("#myElementId").animate({top: 200}).animate({left: 200},{queue:
false});
```

Keep in mind that this also applies to other functions that are in fact wrappers around the `.animate()` function, such as the following:

- `fadeIn()`, `fadeOut()`, and `fadeTo()`
- `hide()` and `show()`
- `slideUp()` and `slideDown()`

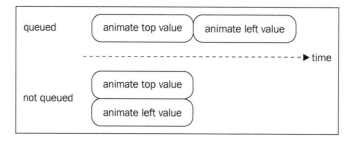

Managing the queue

Here is a list of functions that you can use to manipulate this queue of animations.

.stop()

The .stop() function stops the current animation of the queue. If you provide some more arguments to the call, you can also clear the queue and define if the elements should stop being animated and stay where they are, or jump to their destination.

.clearQueue()

The .clearQueue() function removes all animations from the queue; not only the current one, but also all the next ones.

.dequeue()

The .dequeue() function starts the next animation in the queue. This means that if an animation is being executed when this function is called, then the new one will start as the current one finishes executing. For example, if we take the example at the beginning of this section and add a dequeue() function at the end, the elements will actually start moving diagonally.

```
$("#myElementId")
.animate({top: 200})
.animate({left: 200})
.dequeue();
```

.delay()

The .delay() function allows you to insert a pause between two animations in the queue. For example, if you want to make an element visible with .fadeIn(), then wait for 2 seconds and make it disappear again with .fadeOut(). This would be written like this:

```
$("#myElementId").fadeIn().delay(2000).fadeOut();
```

Other usages of queues

Queues are not used only for animations. When you don't specify otherwise, the queue manipulated by those functions is the fx queue. This is the default queue used by animations. However, if you want to, you could create another queue and add any number of custom functions and delays to script some time-dependent behavior in your game.

Handling of events

If you have used jQuery before, you probably used .click() at some point. It is used to define an event handler that will respond to a mouse click in jQuery. There are many more of those, going from keyboard input, form submission, and window resizing, but we will not go through all these. Instead we will focus on the more "low-level" functions to handle events in jQuery and explain exactly the subtle differences between them.

You would typically use some of those functions to implement the control of your games either with mouse or keyboard inputs.

.bind()

The .bind() function is the basic way to handle events. .click() is, for example, just a wrapper around it. The two lines of the following example have exactly the same effect:

```
$("#myElementId").click(function(){alert("Clicked!")});
$("#myElementId").bind('click', function(){alert("Clicked!")});
```

However, there is a limitation with the usage of bind. Like all other jQuery functions, it only applies to the selected elements. Now, imagine a situation where you want to execute some task each time a user clicks a link with a given class. You would write something like this:

```
$(".myClass").click(function(){/** do something **/});
```

This will work as intended, but only for the link present in the webpage at the moment of its execution. What if you change the content of the page with an Ajax call, and the new content also contains links with this class? You will have to call this line of code again to enhance the new links!

This is far from ideal, because you have to manually track all event handlers you defined that may require to be called again later and all the places where you change the content of the page. This process is very likely to go wrong and you'll end up with some inconsistencies.

The solution to this problem is .delegate(), which is explained in detail in the following section.

.delegate()

With .delegate(), you give the responsibility of handling events to a parent node. This way all elements added later on as a child to this node (directly under it or not) will still see the corresponding handler execute.

The following code fixes the preceding example to make it work with a link added later on. It's implied that all those links are children of a div with the ID attribute as page.

```
$("#page").delegate(
".myClass",
"click",
function(){/** do something **/});
```

This is a very elegant way to solve the problem and it will come in very handy while creating games, for example, where you click on sprites.

Removing event handlers

If you need to remove an event handler you can simply use the .unbind() and .undelegate() functions.

jQuery 1.7

In jQuery 1.7, .delegate() and .bind() have been replaced by .on() (and .off() to remove the handlers). Think of it as a .delegate() function with the capacity to behave like .bind(). If you understand how .delegate() works, you will have no problem to use .on().

Associating data with DOM elements

Let's say you create a div element for each enemy in your game. You will probably want to associate them to some numerical value, like their life. You may even want to associate an object if you're writing object-oriented code.

jQuery provides a simple method to do this, that is, .data(). This method takes a key and a value. If you later call it with only the key, it will return the value. For example, the following code associates the numerical value 3 with the key "numberOfLife" for the element with ID enemy3.

```
$("#enemy3").data("numberOfLife", 3);
```

You may be thinking, "Why shouldn't I simply store my values directly on the DOM element?". There is a very good answer for that. By using .data(), you completely decouple your value and the DOM, which will make it way easier to avoid a situation where the garbage collector doesn't free the memory associated with the DOM of a removed element because you're still holding some cyclic reference to it somewhere.

If you defined some values using the HTML5 data attribute (http://ejohn.org/blog/html-5-data-attributes/), the .data() function retrieves them too.

However, you have to keep in mind that making calls to this function has some performance cost, and if you have many values to store for an element, you may want to store all of them in an object literal associated with a single key instead of many values, each associated with their own key.

Manipulating the DOM

While creating a game with jQuery, you will spend quite some time adding and removing nodes to the DOM. For example, you could create new enemies or remove dead ones. In the next section we'll cover the functions you will be using and we will also see how they work.

.append()

This function allows you to add a child to the currently selected element (or elements). It takes as argument some already existing DOM element, a string containing HTML code that describes an element (or a whole hierarchy of elements), or a jQuery element selecting some nodes. For example, if you wanted to add a child to a node with the ID "content", you would write:

```
$("#content").append("<div>This is a new div!</div>");
```

Keep in mind that if you give a string to this function, the content will have to be parsed and that this could have some performance issues if you do it too often or for very large strings.

.prepend()

This function works exactly like .append(), but adds the new content before the first child of the selected element instead of after its last one.

.html()

This function allows you to completely replace the content of the selected node(s) with the string passed as an argument. If called without an argument, it will return the current HTML content of the first of the selected elements.

If you call it with an empty string, you will erase all the content of the nodes. This could also be achieved by calling `.empty()`.

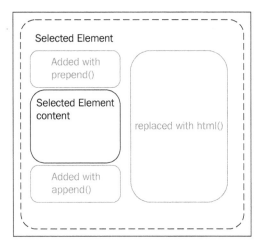

.remove()

This function will simply delete all the selected elements and unregister all the associated event handlers and data.

.detach()

In some situations, you may only want to remove some content for a short period of time and add it again later. This is typically a case where `.remove()` does too much of a good job. What you really want is to keep all those other things you associated with your nodes so that when they get added later on, they will work exactly like before. `.detach()` has been created exactly for this situation. It will behave like `.remove()`, but will allow you to reinsert your elements easily.

Stay curious my friend!

So that's it. I would really encourage you to read the API for each of these functions because there are still some sets of arguments that have not been shown here. If anything is still unclear about any of those functions, don't hesitate to look around the Web for more examples on how to use them. As jQuery is such a popular library, and the Web's culture is one of openness, you will easily find lots of help online.

Here are some places where you can start looking for more information about jQuery:

- jQuery's API: http://api.jquery.com/
- Learning jQuery: http://www.learningjquery.com/

Summary

In this chapter, we've seen some of the most useful jQuery functions for game development and how to use them. By now you should be familiar with the jQuery philosophy and syntax. In the next chapter, we will put what we've learned into practice and create our first game.

2
Creating Our First Game

If you lay your eyes on an electronic device, chances are that there is a browser running on it! You probably have more than one installed on each of your PCs and some more running on your portable devices. If you want to distribute your games to a wide audience for a minimal cost of entry, making it run in the browser makes a lot of sense.

Flash was for a long time the go-to platform for games in browsers, but it has been losing speed in the last few years. There are many reasons for this and there have been countless arguments about whether this is a good thing or not. There is, however, a consensus on the fact that you can now make games run in the browser without plugins at a reasonable speed.

This book will focus on 2D games as they are the ones that run well on current browsers and the features they depend on are standardized. This means that an update of the browser shouldn't break your games and that for the most part you don't have to worry too much about difference between browsers.

You will, however, in the near future be able to develop modern 3D games, like you would on a game console and have them run on browsers. If that's what you thrive on, this book will provide you with fluency in the basic knowledge that you will need to make those games.

In this chapter we will cover the following topics:

- Creating animated sprites
- Moving sprite around
- Preloading assets
- Main game loop implementation using a finite state machine
- Basic collision detection

How does this book work?

Making games has this amazing advantage that you immediately see the result of the code you just wrote move before your eyes. This is the reason why everything you learn in this book will directly be applied to some practical examples. In this chapter, we will write a small game together inspired by the classic *Frogger*. In the following chapters, we will then make a platformer and a role playing game (RPG).

I really encourage you to write your own version of the games presented here and modify the code provided to see the effects it has. There is no better way of learning than to get your hands dirty!

Let's get serious – the game

The game we will implement now is inspired by *Frogger*. In this old school arcade game, you played the role of a frog trying to cross the screen by jumping on logs and avoiding cars.

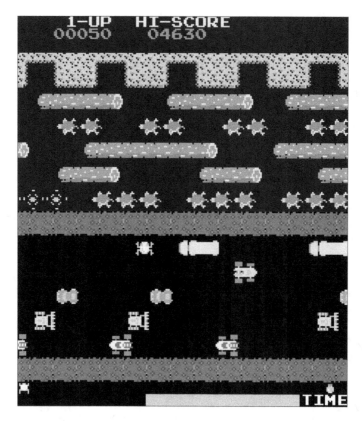

In our version, the player is a developer who has to cross the network cable by jumping packets and then cross the browser "road" by avoiding bugs. To sum up, the game specifications are as follows:

- If the player presses the up arrow key once, the "frog" will go forward one step.

- By pressing the right and left arrow key, the player can move horizontally.

- In the first part (the network cable) the player has to jump on packets coming from the left of the screen and moving to the right. The packets are organized in lines where packets of each line travel at different speeds. Once the player is on a packet, he/she will move along with it. If a packet drives the player outside of the screen, or if the player jumps on the cable without reaching a packet, he/she will die and start at the beginning of the same level once again.

- In the second part (the browser part) the player has to cross the browser screen by avoiding the bugs coming from the left. If the player gets hit by a bug he/she will start at the beginning of the same level once again.

These are very simple rules, but as you will see they will already give us plenty of things to think about.

Learning the basics

Throughout this book, we will use DOM elements to render game elements. Another popular solution would be to use the Canvas element. There are plus and minus points for both technologies and there are a few effects that are simply not possible to produce with only DOM elements.

However, for the beginner, the DOM offers the advantage of being easier to debug, to work on almost all existing browsers (yes, even on Internet Explorer 6), and in most cases to offer reasonable speed for games. The DOM also abstracts the dirty business of having to target individual pixels and tracking which part of the screen has to be redrawn.

Even though Internet Explorer supports most of the features we will see in this book, I would not recommend creating a game that supports it. Indeed, its market share is negligible nowadays (`http://www.ie6countdown.com/`) and you will encounter some performance issues.

Now from some game terminology, sprites are the moving part of a game. They may be animated or nonanimated (in the sense of changing their aspect versus simply moving around). Other parts of the game may include the background, the UI, and tiles (we will look more into this in *Chapter 4, Looking Sideways*).

Framework

During this book, we will write some code; part of the code belongs to an example game and is used to describe scenes or logic that are specific to it. Some code, however, is very likely to be reused in each of your games. For this reason, we will regroup some of those functions into a framework that we will cleverly call `gameFramework` or `gf` in short.

Downloading the example code

You can download the example code files for all Packt books you have purchased from your account at http://www.packtpub.com. If you purchased this book elsewhere, you can visit http://www.packtpub. com/support and register to have the files e-mailed directly to you.

A very simple way to define a namespace in JavaScript is to create an object and add all your function directly to it. The following code gives you an example of what this might look like for two functions, `shake` and `stir`, in the namespace `cocktail`.

```
// define the namespace
var cocktail = {};

// add the function shake to the namespace
cocktail.shake = function(){...}

// add the function stir to the namespace
cocktail.stir = function(){...}
```

This has the advantage of avoiding collision with other libraries that use similar names for their objects or functions. Therefore, from now on when you see any function added to the namespace, it will mean that we think those functions will be used by the other games we will create later in this book or that you might want to create yourself.

The following code is another notation for namespace. Which one you use is a personal preference and you should really use the one that feels right to you!

```
var cocktail = {

    // add the function shake to the namespace
    shake: function(){...},

    // add the function stir to the namespace
    stir: function(){...}
};
```

Typically, you would keep the code of the framework in a JS file (let's say `gameFramework.js`) and the code of the game in another JS file. Once your game is ready to be published, you may want to regroup all your JavaScript code into one file (including jQuery if you wish so) and minimize it. However, for the whole development phase it will be way more convenient to keep them separate.

Sprites

Sprites are the basic building blocks of your game. They are basically images that can be animated and moved around the screen. To create them you can use any image editor. If you work on OS X, there is a free one that I find has been particularly well done, Pixen (`http://pixenapp.com/`).

There are many ways to draw sprites using the DOM. The most obvious one is to use the `img` element. This causes several inconveniences. First, if you want to animate the image you have two options, neither of which are exempt of drawbacks:

- You can use animated gifs. With this method you have no way to access the index of the current frame through JavaScript, and no control over when the animation starts to play or when it ends. Furthermore, having many animated GIFs tends to slow things down a lot.

- You can change the source of the image. This is already a better solution, but provides worse performance if proposed and requires a large number of individual images.

Another disadvantage is that you cannot choose to display only one part of the image; you have to show the entire image each time. Finally, if you want to have a sprite made of a repeating image, you will have to use many `img` elements.

For the sake of completeness, we should mention here one advantage of `img`; it's really easy to scale an `img` element—just adjust the width and height.

The proposed solution uses simple divs of defined dimensions and sets an image in the background. To generate animated sprites, you could change the background image, but instead we use the background position CSS property. The image used in this situation is called a sprite sheet and typically looks something like the following screenshot:

The mechanism by which the animation is generated is shown in the following screenshot:

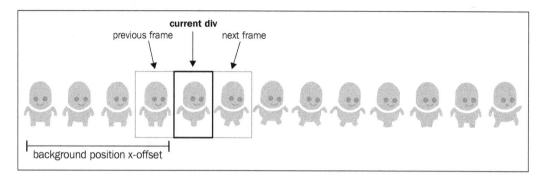

Another advantage is that you can use a single sprite sheet to hold multiple animations. This way you will avoid having to load many different images. Depending on the situation, you may still want to use more than one sprite sheet, but it's a good thing to try to minimize their number.

Implementing animations

It's very simple to implement this solution. We will use `.css()` to change the background properties and a simple `setInterval` to change the current frame of the animation. Therefore, let's say that we have a sprite sheet containing 4 frames of a walk cycle where each frame measures 64 by 64 pixels.

First, we simply have to create a `div` with the sprite sheet as its background. This `div` should measure 64 by 64 pixels, otherwise the next frame would leak onto the current one. In the following example, we add the sprite to a `div` with the ID `mygame`.

```
$("#mygame").append("<div id='sprite1'>");
$("#sprite1").css("backgroundImage","url('spritesheet1.png')");
```

As the background image is by default aligned with the upper-left corner of the `div`, we will only see the first frame of the walk-cycle sprite sheet. What we want is to be able to change what frame is visible. The following function changes the background position to the correct position based on the argument passed to it. Take a look at the following code for the exact meaning of the arguments:

```
/**
 * This function sets the current frame.
 * -divId: the Id of the div from which you want to change the
 *         frame
 * -frameNumber: the frame number
```

```
 *  -frameDimension: the width of a frame
 **/
gameFramework.setFrame = function(divId, frameNumber, frameDimension) {
    $("#"+divId)
        .css("bakgroundPosition", "" + frameNumber * frameDimension +
"px 0px");
}
```

Now we have to call this at regular intervals to produce the animation. We will use `setInterval` with an interval of 60 milliseconds, that is, around 17 frames per second. This should be enough to give the impression of walking; however, this really has to be fine-tuned to match your sprite sheet. To do this we use an anonymous function that we pass to `setInterval`, which will in turn call our function with the correct parameter.

```
var totalNumberOfFrame = 4;
var frameNumber = 0;
setInterval(function(){
    gameFramework.setFrame("sprite1",frameNumber, 64);
    frameNumber = (frameNumber + 1) % totalNumberOfFrame;
}, 60);
```

You probably noticed that we're doing something special to compute the current frame. The goal is to cover values from 0 to 3 (as they're 4 frames) and to loop back to 0 when we reach 4. The operation we use for this is called modulo (%) and it's the rest of the integer division (also known as Euclidean division).

For example, at the third frame we have 3 / 4 which is equal to 0 plus a remainder of 3, so 3 % 4 = 3. When the frame number reaches 4 we have 4 / 4 = 1 plus a remainder of 0, so 4 % 4 = 0. This mechanism is used in a lot of situations.

Adding animations to our framework

As you can see there are more and more variables needed to generate an animation: the URL of the image, the number of frames, their dimension, the rate of the animation, and the current frame. Furthermore, all those variables are associated with one animation, so if we need a second one we have to define twice as many variables.

The obvious solution is to use objects. We will create an animation object that will hold all the variables we need (for now, it won't need any method). This object, like all the things belonging to our framework, will be in the `gameFramework` namespace. Instead of giving all the values of each of the properties of the animation as an argument, we will use a single object literal, and all the properties that aren't defined will default to some well-thought-out values.

To do this, jQuery offers a very convenient method: `$.extend`. This is a very powerful method and you should really take a look at the API documentation (`http://api.jquery.com/`) to see everything that it can do. Here we will pass to it three arguments: the first one will be extended with the values of the second one and the resulting object will be extended with the values of the third.

```
/**
 * Animation Object.
 **/
gf.animation = function(options) {
    var defaultValues = {
        url : false,
        width : 64,
        numberOfFrames : 1,
        currentFrame : 0,
        rate : 30
    };
    $.extend(this, defaultValues, options);
}
```

To use this function we will simply create a new instance of it with the desired values. Here you can see the values used in the preceding examples:

```
var firstAnim = new gameFramework.animation({
    url: "spritesheet1.png",
    numberOfFrames: 4,
    rate: 60
});
```

As you can see, we didn't need to specify `width: 64` because it's the default value! This pattern is very convenient and you should keep it in mind each time you need default values and also the flexibility to override them.

We can rewrite the function to use the animation object:

```
gf.setFrame = function(divId, animation) {
    $("#" + divId)
        .css("bakgroundPosition", "" + animation.currentFrame *
animation.width + "px 0px");
}
```

Now we will create a function for our framework based on the technique we've already seen, but this time it will use the new animation object. This function will start animating a sprite, either once or in a loop. There is one thing we have to be careful about—if we define an animation for a sprite that is already animated we need to deactivate the current animation and replace it with the new one.

To do this we will need an array to hold the list of all intervals' handles. Then we'll only need to check if one exists for this sprite and clear it, then define it again.

```
gf.animationHandles = {};

/**
 * Sets the animation for the given sprite.
 **/
gf.setAnimation = function(divId, animation, loop){
    if(gf.animationHandles[divId]){
        clearInterval(gf.animationHandles[divId]);
    }
    if(animation.url){
        $("#"+divId).css("backgroundImage","url('"+animation.
url+"')");
    }
    if(animation.numberOfFrame > 1){
        gf.animationHandles[divId] = setInterval(function(){
            animation.currentFrame++;
            if(!loop && currentFrame > animation.numberOfFrame){
                clearInterval(gf.animationHandles[divId]);
                gf.animationHandles[divId] = false;
            } else {
                animation.currentFrame %= animation. numberOfFrame;
                gf.setFrame(divId, animation);
            }
        }, animation.rate);
    }
}
```

This will provide a convenient, flexible, and quite high-level way to set an animation for a sprite.

Moving sprites around

Now that we know how to animate a sprite, we need to move it around to make it interesting. A few things are necessary for this; first, the div that we use has to be positioned absolutely. This is very important for two reasons:

- It's a nightmare for the developer to manipulate other positioning as soon as the scene becomes complicated.

- It's by far the least expansive way for the browser to compute the position of an element.

What we want then is the sprite to be positioned relative to the div that holds the game. This means that it too has to be positioned, absolutely, relatively, or fixed.

Once those two conditions are met, we can simply use the `top` and `left` CSS properties to choose where the sprite appears on the screen, as shown in the following screenshot:

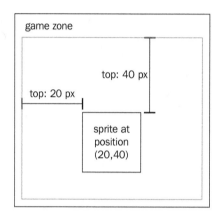

The following code sets the correct parameters for the container div and adds a sprite:

```
$("#mygame").css("position", "relative").append("<div id='sprite1'
style='position: absolute'>");
```

As we will use this piece of code a lot, we will factor it into a function of our framework event if it's trivial. As we did for the animation constructor, we will use an object literal to define the optional arguments.

```
/**
 * This function adds a sprite the div defined by the first argument
 **/
gf.addSprite = function(parentId, divId, options){
    var options = $.extend({
        x: 0,
        y: 0,
        width: 64,
        height: 64
    }, options);

    $("#"+parentId).append("<div id='"+divId+"' style='position:
absolute; left:"+options.x+"px; top: "+options.y+"px; width:
"+options.width+"px ;height: "+options.height+"px'></div>");
}
```

We will then write a function that moves a sprite along the x axis and another one along the y axis. One typical convention in graphic programming is to have the x axis going from left to right and the y axis going from top to bottom. Those functions will take the ID of the element to move and the position to move it to. To mimic the way some jQuery functions work, our functions will return the current position of the sprite if you don't provide a second argument.

```
/**
 * This function sets or returns the position along the x-axis.
 **/
gf.x = function(divId,position) {
    if(position) {
        $("#"+divId).css("left", position);
    } else {
        return parseInt($("#"+divId).css("left"));
    }
}
/**
 * This function sets or returns the position along the y-axis.
 **/
gf.y = function(divId,position) {
    if(position) {
        $("#"+divId).css("top", position);
    } else {
        return parseInt($("#"+divId).css("top"));
    }
}
```

With those three simple functions, you have all the basic tools that you need to generate the graphics of your game.

Preloading

There is, however, one last thing that is required in most cases; asset loading. To avoid starting the game before some of the images are loaded you need to load them before. Most users expect the game to start loading only when they decide to start it. Furthermore, they want some feedback about the progress of the loading process.

In JavaScript, you have the possibility to define, for each image, a function that will be called once the image has finished loading. This, however, has a limitation that it won't provide you with information about the other images. And you can't simply define a callback for the last image that you start to run as you have no guarantee about the order in which your images will load, and in most cases images don't load one after the other, but rather a bunch at a time.

There are many possible solutions, most of them equally good. As this code is run in most cases only once and before the game starts, performance is not of great concern here. What you really want is a robust, flexible system to know when all the images are loaded and the possibility to track the overall progress.

Our solution will use two functions: one to add images to a list of image to preload and the other one to start the preloading.

```
gf.imagesToPreload = [];

/**
 * Add an image to the list of image to preload
 **/
gf.addImage = function(url) {
    if ($.inArray(url, gf.imagesToPreload) < 0) {
        gf.imagesToPreload.push();
    }
    gf.imagesToPreload.push(url);
};
```

This first function doesn't do a lot. It simply takes an URL, checks if it's already present in the array where we store the images to preload, and if the new image is not in the array, add it.

The next function takes two callbacks. The first one is called once all the images are loaded and the second one (if defined) is called with the current progress as a percentage.

```
/**
 * Start the preloading of the images.
 **/
gf.startPreloading = function(endCallback, progressCallback) {
    var images = [];
    var total = gf.imagesToPreload.length;

    for (var i = 0; i < total; i++) {
        var image = new Image();
        images.push(image);
        image.src = gf.imagesToPreload[i];
    }
    var preloadingPoller = setInterval(function() {
        var counter = 0;
        var total = gf.imagesToPreload.length;
```

```
        for (var i = 0; i < total; i++) {
            if (images[i].complete) {
                counter++;
            }
        }
        if (counter == total) {
            //we are done!
            clearInterval(preloadingPoller);
            endCallback();
        } else {
            if (progressCallback) {
                count++;
                progressCallback((count / total) * 100);
            }
        }
    }, 100);
};
```

In this function, we start by defining a new `Image` object for every URL that was added to the list. They will automatically start loading. Then we define a function that we will call at regular intervals. It will use the `complete` properties of images to check if each image is loaded. If the number of loaded images equals the total number of images, it means that we are done preloading.

What could be useful is to automatically add the images used for animations to the preload list. To do this, we just need to add three lines at the end of the animation object in the following way:

```
gf.animation = function(options) {
    var defaultValues = {
        url : false,
        width : 64,
        numberOfFrames : 1,
        currentFrame : 0,
        rate : 30
    };
    $.extend(this, defaultValues, options);
    if(this.url){
        gf.addImage(this.url);
    }
}
```

Initializing the game

The framework part of the game is done. Now we want to implement the graphics and game logic. We can divide the game's code into two parts, one that will be executed only once at the beginning, and one that will be called periodically. We will call the first one the initialization.

This part should be executed as soon as the images are done loading; this is the reason why we will pass it as the end callback for the `startPreloading` function. This means that at the very beginning we need to add all the images that we will use to the preload list. Then once the user launches the game (for example, by clicking an image with the ID `startButton`) we will call the preloader.

The following code uses the standard jQuery way to execute a function once the page is ready. I won't give you the complete code here because some of it is quite repetitive, but I will give at least one example of each of the actions performed here and you can always look at the complete source code if you're curious.

```
$(function() {
    var backgroundAnim = new gf.animation({
        url : "back.png"
    });
    var networkPacketsAnim = new gf.animation({
        url : "packet.png"
    });
    var bugsAnim = new gf.animation({
        url : "bug.png"
    });
    var playerAnim = new gf.animation({
        url : "player.png"
    });

    var initialize = /* we will define the function later */

    $("#startButton").click(function() {
        gf.startPreloading(initialize);
    });
});
```

The following is a list of what we need to do in the initialize function:

- Create the sprites that compose the game scene
- Create the GUI elements

The following diagram shows how we will build our game scene:

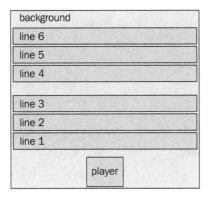

No more than eight sprites: one for the background, one for the player, three for the network packets, and three for the bugs. To make things simpler we will use only one sprite for each band of packets/bugs. The three bands of packets will have the same animation and the same for the three bands of bugs.

To avoid making the elements pop up as they are added, we will first add them to an invisible element and make this element visible only once all the sprites are created.

The only GUI element will be a small div containing the number of lives the player has.

```
var initialize = function() {
    $("#mygame").append("<div id='container' style='display: none;
width: 640px; height: 480px;'>");
    gf.addSprite("container","background",{width: 640, height: 480});
    gf.addSprite("container","packets1",{width: 640, height: 40, y:
400});
    /* and so on */
    gf.addSprite("container","player",{width: 40, height: 40, y: 440,
x: 260});

    gf.setAnimation("background", backgroundAnim);
    gf.setAnimation("player", playerAnim);
    gf.setAnimation("packets1", networkPacketsAnim);
    /* and so on */

    $("#startButton").remove();
    $("#container").append("<div id='lifes' style='position: relative;
color: #FFF;'>life: 3</div>").css("display", "block");
    setInterval(gameLoop, 100);
}
```

The last line of this function is starting the main loop. The main loop is the code that will be executed periodically. It contains most (if not all) of the game logic that doesn't immediately depend on an input from the player.

Main loop

The main loop will typically contain a **finite state machine (FSM)**. An FSM is defined by a series of states and the list of transitions from one state to another. The FSM for a simple game where the player would have to click three boxes that appear one after the other would look like the following diagram:

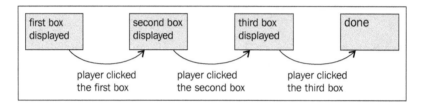

When you implement an FSM, you really need to consider two things: how the game should behave in each state, and what conditions make the game transition to a new state. The advantage of FSMs is that they provide a formal way to organize your game logic. It will make it easier to read your code and you can add/or change your logic at a later time if you need it. I would recommend you to first draw the FSM for your game and keep it somewhere to help you debug your game.

For our *Frogger* game there are 10 states. The initial state is START and the two final states are GAMEOVER and WON. Here is a description of what happens exactly in each state:

- All states: The packets and bugs move to the right
- STARTPOS: Nothing special happens
- LINE1: The player moves at the same speed as the packets of the first line; if the player goes out of the screen it dies and goes back to START
- LINE2: The player moves at the same speed as the packets of the second line, if the player goes out of the screen it dies and goes back to START
- LINE3: The player moves at the same speed as the packets of the third line, if the player goes out of the screen it dies and goes back to START
- REST: Nothing special happens
- LINE4: If the player gets hit by a bug from the line, it dies and goes back to REST

- LINE5: If the player gets hit by a bug from the line, it dies and goes back to REST

- LINE6: If the player gets hit by a bug from the line, it dies and goes back to REST

- WON and GAMEOVER: Nothing special happens

On all states except WON and GAMEOVER the player can move around. This will trigger the following transitions:

- Successful jump: Go to the next state

- Successful left/right slide: Stay in the same state

- Failed jump of left/right slide: If the number of remaining lives is greater than zero, go back to the last "safe" state (START or REST), otherwise transition to GAMEOVER

Main loop implementation

The most readable way to write an FSM is to use switch statements. We will use two, one in the main loop to update the game, and the other in the part that handles keyboard input.

The following code is an extract of the main loop. We first initiate a few variables that we will need to define the behavior of the game, and then code the FSM described in the preceding section. To move the packets and bugs we will use a trick and simply change the background-position. This is a less flexible solution than the function that we wrote earlier, but in this situation it is faster and makes it easy to give the impression of an infinite number of elements with a single sprite.

```
var screenWidth = 640;
var packets1 = {
    position: 300,
    speed: 3
}
/* and so on */

var gameState = "START";

var gameLoop = function() {
    packets1.position += packets1.speed;
    $("#packets1").css("background-position",""+ packets1.position
+"px 0px");
```

```
    /* and so on */

    var newPos = gf.x("player");
    switch(gameState){
        case "LINE1":
            newPos += packets1.speed;
            break;
        case "LINE2":
            newPos += packets2.speed;
            break;
        case "LINE3":
            newPos += packets3.speed;
            break;
    }
    gf.x("player", newPos);
};
```

At this point, the game displays all the moving parts. There still isn't any way for the player to control its avatar. To do this we will use the keydown event handler. We will implement two different solutions to move the sprite around. For the horizontal movement, we will use the gf.x function that we wrote earlier. This makes sense because it's a very small movement, but for the vertical jump we will use $.animate to make the avatar move to its destination in many steps and create a more fluid movement.

```
$(document).keydown(function(e){
    if(gameState != "WON" && gameState != "GAMEOVER"){
        switch(e.keyCode){
            case 37: //left
                gf.x("player",gf.x("player") - 5);
                break;
            case 39: // right
                gf.x("player",gf.x("player") + 5);
                break;
            case 38: // jump
                switch(gameState){
                    case "START":
                        $("#player").animate({top: 400},function()
{

                            gameState = "LINE1";
                        });
                        break;
                    case "LINE1":
                        $("#player").animate({top: 330},function()
{
```

```
                    gameState = "LINE2";
                });
                break;
        /* and so on */
        case "LINE6":
            $("#player").animate({top: 0},function(){
                gameState = "WON";
                $("#lifes").html("You won!");
            });
            break;
    }
  }
 }
});
```

Here we start to check the state of the game to be sure that the player is allowed to move. Then we check which key was pressed. The left and right parts are self-explanatory, but the jump part is subtler.

We need to check the state of the game to find out where the player should jump. Then we use a callback that we pass to the animate function in order to update the state of the game only once the animation is done.

That's it, you can now control the player. If you jump on a packet the player will move with it, and when you reach the end you will win the game. However, you may have noticed we forgot something important: there is no way for the player to die! To add this feature we will need to detect whether the player is at a place that is safe or not.

Collision detection

We will use some sort of collision detection, but a very simple version that is designed only for this situation. In the later chapters, we will see more general solutions, but this isn't necessary here.

There are six spots where collision detection matters in this game; the three lines of packets in the first part, and the three lines of bugs in the second part. Both represent the exact same situation. There is a succession of elements separated by some empty space. The distance between each element is constant along with its size. We don't need to know on which packet the player has jumped or which bugs hit the player, what matters is only if the player stands on a packet or if he/she was hit by a bug.

For this reason we will use the **modulo technique** we used before to reduce the problem complexity. What we will consider is the following situation:

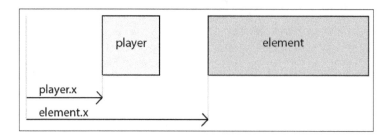

To know if the player touches the element or not we just need to compare its x co-ordinate with the element position.

The following code does just that. First, it checks the game state to know what collision to detect (if any), then uses modulo to bring the player back to the simplified situation we want to consider. And finally, it checks the coordinates of the player.

```
var detectSafe = function(state){
    switch(state){
        case "LINE1":
            var relativePosition = (gf.x("player") - packets1.
position) % 230;
            relativePosition = (relativePosition < 0) ?
relativePosition + 230: relativePosition;
            if(relativePosition > 110 && relativePosition < 210) {
                return true;
            } else {
                return false;
            }
            break;
        /* and so on */
        case "LINE4":
            var relativePosition = (gf.x("player") - bugs1.position) %
190;
            relativePosition = (relativePosition < 0) ?
relativePosition + 190: relativePosition;
            if(relativePosition < 130) {
                return true;
            } else {
                return false;
            }
            break;
```

```
        /* and so on */
    }
    return true;
}
```

There is one small thing you have to be careful about: modulo can have a negative value. This is why we check for this and simply add the width of the repeating part to go back to a positive value.

This is a pretty fast way to detect the solution and there are many such cases where you can design your own collision detection and make it very efficient because you know exactly what to check in your particular situation.

Now we can call this method in our game. There are two places where this should be done: in the main loop and in the input handler. When we detect that the player died, we need to decrease its life and move it to the right place. Furthermore, we want to detect that the player has no more life and change the game's state to GAMEOVER in this situation. The following function does just that:

```
var life = 3;
var kill = function (){
    life--;
    if(life == 0) {
        gameState = "GAMEOVER";
        $("#lifes").html("Game Over!");
    } else {
        $("#lifes").html("life: "+life);
        switch(gameState){
            case "START":
            case "LINE1":
            case "LINE2":
            case "LINE3":
                gf.x("player", 260);
                gf.y("player", 440);
                gameState = "START";
                break;
            case "REST":
            case "LINE4":
            case "LINE5":
            case "LINE6":
                gf.x("player", 260);
                gf.y("player", 220);
                gameState = "REST";
                break;
        }
    }
}
```

Now we can add the collision detection in the main loop. We will need to check for another thing: the player shouldn't go out of the screen in one of the packets.

```
var newPos = gf.x("player");
switch(gameState){
    case "LINE1":
        newPos += packets1.speed;
        break;
    /* and so on */
}
if(newPos > screenWidth || newPos < -40){
        kill();
} else {
    if(!detectSafe(gameState)){
        kill();
    }
    gf.x("player", newPos);
}
```

In the input handler, we will add the code into the callback executed at the end of the jump animation. For example, to check collision for a jump from the start to the first line we will write the following:

```
case "START":
    $("#player").animate({top: 400},function(){
        if(detectSafe("LINE1")){
            gameState = "LINE1";
        } else {
            kill();
        }
    });
    break;
```

Here you see why we didn't use gameState in the kill function. In this situation, the player is still in its previous state. It still hasn't "landed" so to say.
Only if the jump was safe, we will change the player's state to the next line.

Summary

We now have a game that completely implements the specification that we defined at the beginning of the chapter. The code is not yet optimized and that will be the subject of our next chapter, but to make a game that is nice to play it would really need more polish. You could add a high-score system, integration with social networks, and sound and touch device compatibility.

We will cover those topics and more in the future chapters. However, there are a lot of things you can do with what you have already learned now to make the game better: you may want to add an animation for when the player dies, a nicer GUI, nicer graphics, the ability to jump back, and more than one level. It's these small things that will make your game stand out and you should really invest a big part of your time to give this professional finish to your game!

3
Better, Faster, but not Harder

The game we just developed will work just fine on almost all devices and in almost all browsers, the main reason being it's very simple and contains few moving sprites. However, as soon as you'll try to make a more complex game like we will in the following chapters, you'll realize that you need to take great care to write optimized code for obtaining good performance.

In this chapter, we will look back at our previous code and propose an optimized version of some of its aspects. Some of those optimizations are there to make your game run faster and some others are there to make your code more readable and easier to maintain.

In general, it's a good practice to implement a first version of your game with fewer features without worrying too much about performance, and then optimize and add more functions to it. This helps you to avoid spending too much time on something you may not need in the game, allowing you to benchmark your optimizations to make sure they really make things faster, and most importantly, keep you motivated.

In this chapter, we will dive deeper into the following areas:

- Reducing the number of intervals and timeouts
- Keyboard polling
- Using HTML fragments
- Avoiding reflow
- Using CSS Transform to speed up sprite positioning
- Using `requestAnimationFrame` instead of timeouts

Intervals and timeouts

In our game we used a lot of `setInterval` calls. You may think that those calls are multithreaded, but they are not. JavaScript is strictly single-threaded (with the recent exception of WebWorkers, but we won't look into that here). This means that all those calls are really run one after the other.

If you're interested in the dirty details of how exactly intervals and timeouts work, I would recommend reading the excellent article written by *John Resig, How JavaScript Timers Work* (`http://ejohn.org/blog/how-javascript-timers-work/`).

Therefore, intervals and timeouts don't add multithreading to your code, and there are many reasons why you may want to avoid using them too much. First, it makes your code somewhat difficult to debug. Indeed, depending on how much time each call takes, your interval will be executed in a different order, and even those will be of the exact same periodicity.

Furthermore, performance-wise, using `setInterval` and `setTimeout` too much can be very taxing on older browsers.

The alternative is to use a single interval to replace all your animation's functions and the game loop.

One interval to rule them all

Using one single interval doesn't necessarily mean that you want all your animations to execute at the same rate. An acceptable solution in most cases is to allow any multiple of the base interval for the animations.

Typically, you will have your game loop running at a given rate (let's say 30 milliseconds), and your animations running at the same rate or two, three, four times slower. However, this doesn't have to be restricted to animations; you may want to have more than one game loop, some of them executed at a much lower rate.

For example, you may want to increase the level of the water in a platform game every second. That way, the player has the incentive to finish the level quickly, otherwise he/she will drown. To allow this in the framework, we will add an `addCallback` function that will take a function and a rate. The game loop from our previous game will be implemented using this instead of `setInterval`.

This means that the `startPreloading` function will slightly change. After the call to the `endCallback` function, we will start a `setInterval` function with a new function that will call all the functions that have been defined through `addCallback` and take care of the animations. Furthermore, we will change its name simply to `startGame` to reflect the change in usage.

In the game, it won't be necessary to explicitly create an interval with the game loop as this is automatically done by the startGame function; we just have to add it to the game with the function addCallback. The following image shows a comparison of this method and the one using many setTimeout functions:

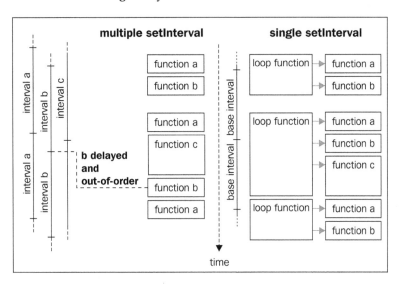

We will implement this in our framework by providing this minimal refresh rate to an initialize function. From this point, all the animations and periodical functions will be defined as a multiple of it. We will still use milliseconds in the API to describe their rate, but will store the rate internally as the closest multiple of the base rate.

Code

Our initialize function will use the $.extend function that we used. For now on, we will only have the base refresh rate, but we will add more values as we need them. We also need to define the default values for the base refresh rate to account for the situation where the user didn't specify one manually.

```
gf = {
    baseRate: 30
};

gf.initialize = function(options) {
    $.extend(gf, options);
}
```

The newly renamed `startGame` function will look like the following code:

```
gf.startGame = function(progressCallback) {
    /* ... */
    var preloadingPoller = setInterval(function() {
        /* ... */
        if (counter == total) {
            //we are done!
            clearInterval(preloadingPoller);
            endCallback();
            setInterval(gf.refreshGame, gf.baseRate);
        } else {
            /* ... */
        }
    }, 100);
};
```

We didn't change much here; after the `endCallback` function, we added a call to an internal function: `gf.refreshGame`. It's this function that will, in turn, coordinate both the refreshment of animations and periodic function calls.

This new function will use two lists to know when to do what, one for callbacks and one for animations. We have one for animations already: `gf.animationHandles`. We will rename it simply to `gf.animations` and create a second one named `gf.callbacks`.

Both lists will have to include a way to know if they should be executed at the current iteration of the base rate or not. To detect this, we will use a simple counter for each animation and callback. Each time the base loop executes, we will increment all of them and compare their values with the rate of the associate animation/callback. If they are equal, it means that we need to execute it and reset the counter.

```
gf.refreshGame = function (){
    // update animations
    var finishedAnimations = [];

    for (var i=0; i < gf.animations.length; i++) {

        var animate = gf.animations[i];

        animate.counter++;
        if (animate.counter == animate.animation.rate) {
            animate.counter = 0;
            animate.animation.currentFrame++;
```

```
                   if(!animate.loop && animate.animation.currentFrame >
       animate.animation.numberOfFrame) {
                        finishedAnimations.push(i);
                   } else {
                        animate.animation.currentFrame %= animate.animation.
       numberOfFrame;
                        gf.setFrame(animate.div, animate.animation);
                   }
              }
         }
         for(var i=0; i < finishedAnimations.length; i++){
              gf.animations.splice(finishedAnimations[i], 1);
         }

         // execute the callbacks
         for (var i=0; i < gf.callbacks.length; i++) {
              var call  = gf.callbacks[i];

              call.counter++;
              if (call.counter == call.rate) {
                   call.counter = 0;
                   call.callback();
              }
         }
    }
}
```

This simple mechanism will replace the many calls to setInterval and solve the problems associated to this that we mentioned earlier.

The function that sets animations to a div has to be adapted in consequence. As you've seen in the preceding example, the actual code that takes care of finding out which frame of the animation has to be defined is now in the refreshGame function. This means that the setAnimation function just needs to add the animation to the list without caring about how it will be animated.

The part of the function that checks if the div already has an animation associated to it is now slightly more complicated, but otherwise the function is now much simpler.

gf.animations = [];

```
   /**
    * Sets the animation for the given sprite.
    **/
   gf.setAnimation = function(divId, animation, loop){
       var animate = {
     animation: animation,
```

```
        div: divId,
            loop: loop,
            counter: 0
        }

        if(animation.url){
            $("#"+divId).css("backgroundImage","url('"+animation.
url+"')");
        }

        // search if this div already has an animation
        var divFound = false;
        for (var i = 0; i < gf.animations.length; i++) {
            if(gf.animations[i].div == divId){
                divFound = true;
                gf.animations[i] = animate
            }
        }

        // otherwise we add it to the array
        if(!divFound) {
            gf.animations.push(animate);
        }
    }
```

We need to write a similar code to add the callbacks to the base loop:

```
gf.callbacks = [];

gf.addCallback = function(callback, rate){
    gf.callbacks.push({
        callback: callback,
        rate: Math.round(rate / gf.baseRate),
        counter: 0
    });
}
```

This function is trivial; the only interesting part is the normalization of the refresh rate to express it as a multiple of the base rate. You probably noticed that we didn't do anything of that sort for animations, but we will do this now in the function that creates animations. It will now look like this:

```
gf.animation = function(options) {
    var defaultValues = {
        url : false,
        width : 64,
```

```
            numberOfFrames : 1,
            currentFrame : 0,
            rate : 1
        }
        $.extend(this, defaultValues, options);
        if(options.rate){
            // normalize the animation rate
            this.rate = Math.round(this.rate / gf.baseRate);
        }
        if(this.url){
            gf.addImage(this.url);
        }
    }
```

And that's it; with those simple changes, we will get rid of most `setInterval` functions. It may seem quite a lot of work to duplicate functionality that you get out of the box with vanilla JavaScript, but you will see in time that it helps quite a lot when you start debugging your game.

Keyboard polling

If you played the game from the last chapter, you may have noticed that the movements from left to right from our "frog" are somewhat strange, that is, if you press and hold the left key, your avatar will move left a bit, stall for some time, and start moving left continually.

This behavior is not directly caused by the browser, but rather by the operating system. What's happening here is that the OS will repeat any key when it stays pressed long enough (also known as "sticky keys"). There are two parameters that define this behavior:

- The grace period: This is the time during which the OS will wait before repeating the keys. This avoids repeating the keys when you really mean to press them once.
- The frequency at which the keys will repeat.

You have no control on those parameters or on the occurrence of this behavior. It all depends on the OS and the way the user configured it.

For continuous actions, this is far from ideal. If you move an avatar around in an RPG or a platformer game, you need the movement to be continuous and linear in speed. A solution to this problem is called state polling. With this method, you want to actively query the state of some keys instead of waiting for a change in state as is done with event handling.

In your game loop, you would at some point ask if the key "left" is pressed and react accordingly. This is used a lot in native games, but JavaScript doesn't offer this possibility out of the box. We will have to implement a state polling technique ourselves.

Keeping track of the keys' state

To do this we will use the only tools available: the `keydown` and `keyup` events. We will register two event handlers:

1. If a key with a given keycode "c" is pressed, the first event handler will write `true` in an array at index "c".

2. When the same key is released, the second event handler sets the value of index "c" to `false`.

A nice feature of this solution is that we don't need to initialize the state of the array for each possible key as, by default, it is undefined; so, when we check, its value will return `false`. The following image illustrates how these two event handlers work:

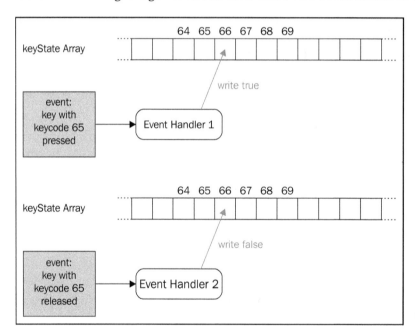

We will register those two event handlers at the end of our framework:

```
gf.keyboard = [];
// keyboard state handler
  $(document).keydown(function(event){
```

```
        gf.keyboard[event.keyCode] = true;
});
$(document).keyup(function(event){
        gf.keyboard[event.keyCode] = false;
});
```

Once this is done, we can simply move the code that handles the left and right movement to our game loop and rewrite it to use the `gf.keyboard` array.

```
if(gf.keyboard[37]){ //left
        newPos -= 5;
}
if(gf.keyboard[39]){ //right
        newPos += 5;
}
```

Here we don't need to check if the player dies because we already do it once in the game loop. You just have to keep in mind that more than one key can be pressed at the same time. This wasn't the case in the previous version that used an event handler and where one event was generated for each key that was pressed.

If you try the game now, you will notice that the horizontal movements of your player are much better.

As you can see, the code that uses polling is prettier and in most cases more compact. Furthermore, it is inside the game loop, which is always a good thing. However, there are still situations where it may not be the best solution. Making our frog jump is a perfect example of this.

Choosing between event handling and polling really depends on the situation, but in general, if you want to react to a key pressed once you will use events, and if you want to react to a key pressed continuously you will use polling.

HTML fragments

Here we will look at some small optimizations in the code that creates the sprites. As this function is called only eight times in our entire game and only during the initialization phase, it's not very important that it's fast in this case. However, there are many situations where you need to create lots of sprites during the game, for example, when shooting lasers in a shoot-'em-up when creating levels of a platformer or the maps of an RPG.

This technique avoids parsing the HTML code (that describes a sprite) each time that you add one to the game. It uses what's called an HTML fragment, which is a kind of a severed branch from the usual HTML tree of nodes.

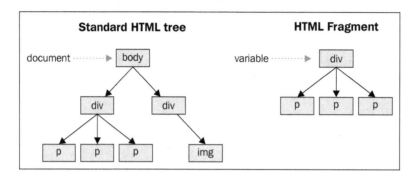

jQuery offers a very simple way to generate such a fragment:

```
var fragment = $("<div>fragment</div>");
```

In this example, the variable `fragment` will hold the HTML element in memory until we need to use it. It is not automatically added to the document. If you want to add it later you can simply write:

```
$("#myDiv").append(fragment);
```

Keep in mind that the fragment is still referencing the added element, which means that if you add it to another location later on it will be removed from the previous one, and if you modify it you will modify the document too.

To avoid this situation, what you want is to clone the fragment before you insert it into your document, as shown in the following code:

```
$("#myDiv").append(fragment.clone());
```

This is exactly the way we will rewrite our `addSprite` function to make it faster:

```
gf.spriteFragment = $("<div style='position: absolute'></div>");
gf.addSprite = function(parentId, divId, options){
    var options = $.extend({}, {
        x: 0,
        y: 0,
        width: 64,
        height: 64
    }, options);
    $("#"+parentId).append(gf.spriteFragment.clone().css({
```

```
        left:    options.x,
        top:     options.y,
        width:   options.width,
        height:  options.height}).attr("id",divId));
};
```

Here we created a fragment for the only part that is common to every sprite. Then, before we add it to the document, we clone it and add the special parameters that were provided to the `addSprite` function, such as its position, size, and ID.

Like I said before, you probably won't have noticed any visible changes for our very simple game, but this code is much more efficient and will come in handy in more complex games where we generate lots of sprites.

Avoiding reflow

When modifying the DOM, you must try to avoid generating a complete reflow of the whole document, or of a large part of it. There are many ways of minimizing the risk of doing this, and modern browsers are pretty good at optimizing when they do it.

Typically, the browser will try to regroup as much modification it can before reflowing the document. However, if you try to access information that is dependent on one of those modifications, it will have to perform a reflow in order to be able to calculate the new information.

A pretty good rule of thumb is to avoid reading the DOM, like the plague, and as a last resort, group all reads and perform them at the end of the refresh loop.

In our game there is one point where we are in this exact situation: Each time we access the X position of the player's avatar, we force the browser to reflow. Position and size is probably the most frequently accessed information during the game loop. One simple way to make things faster is to avoid getting them from the DOM. Indeed, as long as they are set through the framework function, we can simply store them somewhere and retrieve them when needed.

To do this we will use jQuery's `data` function to associate our sprite with an object literal containing those interesting values. The `addSprite` function would be extended this way:

```
gf.addSprite = function(parentId, divId, options){
    /* ... */
    $("#"+parentId).append(gf.spriteFragment.clone().css({
            left:    options.x,
            top:     options.y,
```

```
                width:  options.width,
                height: options.height}).attr("id",divId).
    data("gf",options));
    }
```

Then, in the gf.x and gf.y functions we will use this value instead of the CSS property:

```
gf.x = function(divId,position) {
    if(position) {
        $("#"+divId).css("left", position);
        $("#"+divId).data("gf").x = position;
    } else {
        return $("#"+divId).data("gf").x;
    }
}
gf.y = function(divId,position) {
    if(position) {
        $("#"+divId).css("top", position);
        $("#"+divId).data("gf").y = position;
    } else {
        return $("#"+divId).data("gf").y;
    }
}
```

This also has the advantage of getting rid of two parseInt values, and the code of the game doesn't even have to change!

Moving your sprite around using CSS Transforms

Using CSS Transforms is a simple hack that allows you to move objects on the screen much faster than it does with the use of CSS top and left properties. If you decide to use this, you have to be aware that not all browsers support it.

We won't go into too much detail because CSS Transforms are explained in the next chapter, *Looking Sideways*. The following code is the modification required to use CSS Transforms:

```
gf.x = function(divId,position) {
    if(position) {
        var data = $("#"+divId).data("gf");
        var y = data.y;
        data.x = position;
```

```
        $("#"+divId).css("transform", "translate("+position+"px,
"+y+"px)");
    } else {
        return $("#"+divId).data("gf").x;
    }
}
gf.y = function(divId,position) {
    if(position) {
        var data = $("#"+divId).data("gf");
        var x = data.x;
        data.y = position;
        $("#"+divId).css("transform", "translate("+x+"px,
"+position+"px)");
    } else {
        return $("#"+divId).data("gf").y;
    }
}
```

As you can see in the highlighted part of the code, we need to set both coordinates each time. This means that we have to retrieve the y coordinate when we modify the x coordinate and vice versa.

Using requestAnimationFrame instead of timeouts

A new feature has been added quite recently to browsers in order to make animations smoother: requestAnimationFrame. This makes the browser tell you when it's the best possible time to animate your page instead of doing it whenever you feel like it. You would use this instead of registering your callbacks with setInterval or setTimeout.

When you use requestAnimationFrame, it's the browser that decides when it will call the function. Therefore, you'll have to take into account the exact time that passed since the last call. The standard specification used to define this time is milliseconds (like the ones you would get with Date.now()), but it's now given by a high-precision timer.

As there are implementations of those two versions around, and this feature is vendor-prefixed in most browsers, you should use a tool to abstract the dirty details. I would recommend reading these two articles, both of which provide code snippets that you could use:

- `http://paulirish.com/2011/requestanimationframe-for-smart-animating/`
- `http://www.makeitgo.ws/articles/animationframe/`

Summary

In this chapter, we spent some time optimizing the game we wrote in *Chapter 2, Creating Our First Game*. We've seen some optimization techniques that will make our game smoother without impacting our game's code readability.

The framework we've built is now a reasonable foundation upon which we can build a more complete one in the following chapters. We will begin in the following one by adding the capability to create tile maps that we will use to implement a platformer game.

4
Looking Sideways

It's now time to make a more complex game. We will implement a very popular genre, that of the 2D platform game. Some early examples of this genre are *Super Mario Bros* and *Sonic the Hedgehog*. These games are typically built using small repetitive sprites, called tile maps, for the level design. We will add these, as well as a more general collision detection, to our framework. For the game logic itself we will use object-oriented code.

Here is a quick list of the features we will have to add to our framework:

- Offline divs
- Groups
- Sprite transformation
- Tile maps
- Collision detections

We will first begin by going through all of these, and will then start with the game.

Offline divs

As explained at the end of the previous chapter, avoiding reflow is a good way to speed things up. It's not always easy to completely avoid querying the state of the DOM during your manipulations. And even if you are very careful, as a framework developer, you are never sure what the user of your framework will do. However, there is a way to reduce the negative effect of a reflow; detach the piece of DOM you are working on, modify it, and then attach it back to the document.

Let's say you have a node with the ID box and want to manipulate its child elements in a complex manner. The following code shows you how to detach it:

```
// detach box
var box = $("#box").detach();

var aSubElement = box.find("#aSubElement")
// and so on

// attach it back
box.appendTo(boxParent);
```

This requires a small modification of our framework's API; until now, we used a string to identify sprites. This has the side effect of requiring the sprite to be part of the document. For example, if you call gf.x("sprite"), jQuery will try to find a node with the ID sprite in the document. If you detach the sprite or one of its parents,
the function won't find its ID.

The solution is simply to provide the DOM node itself to our framework's functions. As we use jQuery, we will wrap this node in jQuery. Let's compare the current API and the proposed one for the gf.x function.

```
// current API
var xCoordinate = gf.x("mySprite");

// proposed API
var xCoordinate = gf.x($("#mySprite"));
```

This solution has another advantage; it allows for further optimization. If we look at the implementation of this function, we will find another problem:

```
gf.x = function(divId,position) {
    if(position) {
        $("#"+divId).css("left", position);
        $("#"+divId).data("gf").x = position;
    } else {
        return $("#"+divId).data("gf").x;
    }
}
```

You can see that each time the function is called, jQuery is used to retrieve the element. Any access to the DOM (even using the element's ID in the selector) to find the element has a performance cost. Ideally, if the concerned element is used more than a few times, you may want to cache it to improve performance. This is made possible with the proposed API.

The implementation is pretty straightforward, so we will only show the `gf.x` function:

```
gf.x = function(div,position) {
    if(position) {
        div.css("left", position);
        div.data("gf").x = position;
    } else {
        return div.data("gf").x;
    }
}
```

Groups

It's very convenient to organize the elements of your game in a hierarchical manner. A typical game could be organized this way:

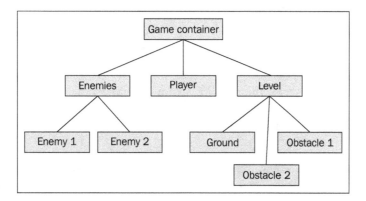

To allow this, we need to add a very simple thing called groups to our framework. A group is basically a simple div, positioned exactly like a sprite, but has no background and no width and height. We will add a `gf.addGroup` function to do this for us. Its signature will be the same as that of `gf.addSprite`, but the options argument will only hold *x* and *y* coordinates.

The following example shows you how to generate the tree shown in the previous figure:

```
var enemies    = gf.addGroup(container,"enemies");
var enemy1     = gf.addSprite(group,"enemy1",{...});
var enemy2     = gf.addSprite(group,"enemy2",{...});

var player     = gf.addSprite(group,"player",{...});
```

```
var level     = gf.addGroup(container,"level");
var ground    = gf.addSprite(group,"ground",{...});
var obstacle1 = gf.addSprite(group,"obstacle1",{...});
var obstacle2 = gf.addSprite(group,"obstacle2",{...});
```

The implementation of this function is very similar to that of gf.addSprite:

```
gf.groupFragment = $("<div style='position: absolute; overflow:
visible;'></div>");
gf.addGroup = function(parent, divId, options){
    var options = $.extend({
        x: 0,
        y: 0,
    }, options);
    var group = gf.groupFragment.clone().css({
            left:    options.x,
            top:     options.y}).attr("id",divId).data("gf",options);
    parent.append(group);
    return group;
}
```

Having multiple entities on our game screen makes it necessary to have a simple way to differentiate between them. We could use a flag in the object literal associated with the node through the $.data function, but we will instead use CSS classes. This has the advantage of making it very easy to retrieve or filter all the elements of one type.

To implement this, we just have to change the fragments for sprites and groups. The name we will give to the CSS class will be namespaced. Namespacing in CSS is simply done with a prefix in the class name. For example, we will give our sprites the class gf_sprite; this will minimize the chance that another plugin uses the same class, in contrast to, say, sprite.

The new fragment will look like this:

```
gf.spriteFragment = $("<div class='gf_sprite' style='position:
absolute; overflow: hidden;'></div>");
gf.groupFragment = $("<div class='gf_group' style='position: absolute;
overflow: visible;'></div>");
```

Now if you want to find all the children that are sprites, you can write something like this:

```
$("#someElement").children(".gf_sprite");
```

Sprite transformation

There are many situations where you will want to transform your sprites in simple ways. You may want, for example, to make them bigger or smaller or to rotate or flip them. The most convenient method for doing this is by using CSS transforms. In the last few years, CSS transforms have become well supported by most browsers.

If you decide to use this feature, you just have to realize that versions before Microsoft Internet Explorer 9 do not support it. There is the possibility to use the proprietary `filter` CSS property, but in most cases, it's way too slow.

Another possibility is that of using a technique used in some of the old 8-bit and 16-bit games. You can simply generate the images for the transformed sprite. This has the advantage of being very fast and being compatible with all browsers. On the other hand, it will increase the size of your artworks and requires you to regenerate all the transformations if you need to change your sprite at some point.

We will here only implement the CSS transform solution because in most situations it's acceptable to target modern browsers only.

CSS transform

There are many transformations that are possible in CSS, even 3D ones (you can take a look at `https://github.com/boblemarin/Sprite3D.js` for some very good examples of this), but we will stick to rotation and scaling.

In most browsers, the CSS property "transform" is vendor prefixed. This means that in Safari, for example, it will be called `-webkit-transform`, and in Firefox, `-moz-transform`. Working with properties of this kind used to be a real pain, but with jQuery 1.8, you can simply forget about it and act as if there was no prefix. jQuery will take care of using the correct prefix where it needs it.

As explained before, there are many values that this property can take, and we will focus on two here: `rotate` and `scale`. The syntax for `rotate` is as follows:

```
transform: rotate(angle)
```

Here, `angle` is a clockwise angle expressed with its unit, either degrees or radians (abbreviated respectively as **deg** and **rad**). The rotation is done around the origin of the element, by default, its center. This is what you want in a game most of the time, but if you want to change it for some reason, you can simply use the `transform-origin` CSS properties to do so.

For example, if you want to rotate your element 10 degrees counterclockwise you would write:

```
transform: rotate(-10deg);
```

It would look like this if your element were a red square:

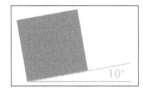

The way `scale` works is very similar, but it has two possible syntaxes:

- `transform: scale(ratio)`
- `transform: scale(ratio_x, ratio_y)`

If you specify only one value, the result will be an isotropic transformation; in other words, of equal magnitude along both axes. On the contrary, if you specify two values, the first will scale along the x axis and the second one along the y axis (anisotropic transformation). The following figure illustrates the difference between those two.

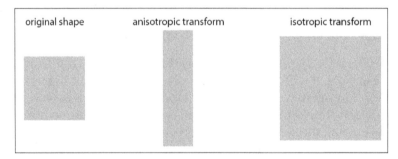

In our case, we will not include arbitrary anisotropic scaling into our framework, but we will still use the two-value syntax because it will allow us to flip our sprites; indeed, if we write `scale(-1,1)`, this will in effect mean "flip the element along the x axis (horizontally) and leave it unchanged along the y axis". Of course, this works with values other than 1; as long as the magnitude of the two values is the same, you will only flip the sprite and not change its aspect ratio.

These two values for the transform property work well together, so if you wanted to rotate an element 10 degrees counterclockwise, flip it vertically, and make it twice as large, you would write:

```
transform: rotate(-10deg) scale(2,-2);
```

Adding transform to the framework

Now we have to write a function that does this for us. As with most of our framework's functions, we will use an object literal to hold the optional arguments and give the node to which the function applies as a first argument. A call to this function to generate the example is as follows:

```
gf.transform (myDiv, {rotate: -10, scale: 2, flipV: true});
```

The angle is in degrees and the `flipH` and `flipV` options are Boolean values. The values of the omitted parameters (`flipH`, in this example) won't default to a general value; what we will do instead is to take the current value of this parameter for the given element. This will allow you to call the transform function twice and change two different parameters without having to know what the other call is doing. For example:

```
gf.transform (myDiv, {rotate: -10});
// do some other things
gf.transform (myDiv, {scale: 2, flipV: true});
```

This will, however, mean that we won't be able to use the `$.extend` function like we used to. Instead, we will have to manually check the stored value of the undefined parameters for the given elements.

These values will be stored in the object literal associated with the `gf` key, which is associated with our element that has the `$.data` function. That also means that we will need to define the default value for those properties when we create the sprite (or group). For example, the `addSprite` function will start with:

```
gf.addSprite = function(parent, divId, options){
    var options = $.extend({
        x: 0,
        y: 0,
        width: 64,
        height: 64,
        flipH: false,
        flipV: false,
        rotate: 0,
        scale: 1
    }, options);
//...
```

Once you've understood the way in which the CSS `transform` property works, the implementation of our `gf.transform` function will be pretty straightforward:

```
gf.transform = function(div, options){
    var gf = div.data("gf");
    if(options.flipH !== undefined){
        gf.flipH = options.flipH;
    }
    if(options.flipV !== undefined){
        gf.flipV = options.flipV;
    }
    if(options.rotate !== undefined){
        gf.rotate = options.rotate;
    }
    if(options.scale !== undefined){
        gf.scale = options.scale;
    }
    var factorH = gf.flipH ? -1 : 1;
    var factorV = gf.flipV ? -1 : 1;
    div.css("transform", "rotate("+gf.rotate+"deg) scale("+(gf.
scale*factorH)+","+(gf.scale*factorV)+")");
}
```

Once again, this is a simple function that will provide great functionality and allow us to create neat effects in our games. Depending on your game, you may want to add the anisotropic scaling to it or even 3D transform, but the basic structure and API of the function can remain the same.

Tile maps

Tile maps are a very common tool for making lots of games. The idea behind it is that most levels are made of similar parts. The ground, for example, is likely to repeat itself a lot, with a few variations; there will be a few kinds of different trees repeated many times, and a few items such as stones and flowers or grass will appear many times, represented by the exact same sprite.

This means that using one big image to describe your level is not the most efficient solution size-wise. What you really want is to be able to give a list of all the unique elements and then describe how they are combined to generate your level.

Tile maps are the simplest implementation of this. They add a constraint though; all elements must be of the same size and placed on a grid. If you can work with those constraints, this solution becomes very efficient; that's the reason why so many old games were created with it.

We will start by implementing a very naive version of it and then show, at the end of the chapter, how we can make it faster in most situations without too much work.

To sum up, a tile map is made up of:

- A series of images (what we call animations in our framework)
- A bi-dimensional array describing what image goes where

The following figure illustrates this:

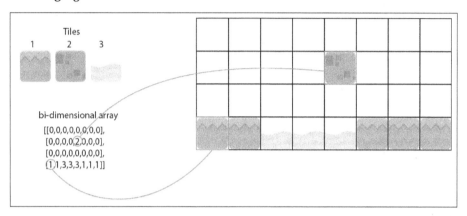

In addition to being useful for reducing the size of your game, tile maps offer the following advantages:

- Detecting collisions with a tile map is very easy.
- The array that describes how the tile map looks also contains semantic information about the level. For example, tiles 1 to 3 are ground tiles, while 4 to 6 are part of the scenery also. This will allow you to easily "read" the level and react to it.
- It's very simple to generate random variation of levels. Just create the bi-dimensional array with a few rules, and your game will be different each time the player starts again!
- Lots of open-source tools exist that help you create them.

However, you have to realize that there are some constraints too:

- As all the elements composing the tile map have the same size, if you want to create a bigger element, you will have to decompose it into smaller parts, which could be tedious.
- Even if done with a lot of talent, it will give a certain continual look to your game. If you want to avoid having some blocks that repeat around your level, tile maps are not for you.

Naive implementation

We already know how to create a sprite, so basically what we need in order to create a tile map is to generate the sprites that compose it. Just like `gf.addSprite`, our `gf.addTilemap` function will take the parent div, the ID of the generated tile map, and an object literal describing the options.

The options are the position of the tile map, the dimension of each tile, and the number of tiles that compose the tile map horizontally and vertically, the list of animations, and the bi-dimensional array describing the tile position.

We will iterate through the bi-dimensional array and create the sprite as needed. It's often convenient to have places without sprites in our tile map, so we will use the following conventions:

- If all the entries have zeroes, it means that no sprites need to be created at this place
- If all the places have a number greater than zero, it means that a sprite with an animation at the index corresponding to this number minus one in the animation array should be created

This is typically a place where you want to create your complete tile map before adding it to the document. We will use a cloned fragment to generate the `div` tag holding all the tiles and add to it the cloned fragment we used for sprites too. Only once all the tiles are created will we add the tile map to the document.

There is one more subtlety here. We will add two classes to our tiles, one that marks which columns the tile belong to, and another that marks which row it belongs to. Other than that, there are no big subtleties in the code for now:

```
gf.tilemapFragment = $("<div class='gf_tilemap' style='position:
absolute'></div>");
gf.addTilemap = function(parent, divId, options){
    var options = $.extend({
        x: 0,
        y: 0,
        tileWidth: 64,
        tileHeight: 64,
        width: 0,
        height: 0,
        map: [],
        animations: []
    }, options);
```

```
        //create line and row fragment:
    var tilemap = gf.tilemapFragment.clone().attr("id",divId).
data("gf",options);
    for (var i=0; i < options.height; i++){
        for(var j=0; j < options.width; j++) {
            var animationIndex = options.map[i][j];

            if(animationIndex > 0){
                var tileOptions = {
                    x: options.x + j*options.tileWidth,
                    y: options.y + i*options.tileHeight,
                    width: options.tileWidth,
                    height: options.tileHeight
                }
                var tile = gf.spriteFragment.clone().css({
                    left:   tileOptions.x,
                    top:    tileOptions.y,
                    width:  tileOptions.width,
                    height: tileOptions.height}
                ).addClass("gf_line_"+i).addClass("gf_column_"+j).
data("gf", tileOptions);

                gf.setAnimation(tile, options.
animations[animationIndex-1]);

                tilemap.append(tile);
            }
        }
    }
    parent.append(tilemap);
    return tilemap;
}
```

That's it for now. This will generate the whole tile map at initialization time. This means that very large tile maps will be slow. We will see at the end of the chapter how to generate only the part of the tile map that is visible.

Collision detection

This is a very important part of our framework, and we will start by looking at how we will do this for the case of a sprite colliding with the tile map. This situation has the advantage of being easier than the general case, but still using most of the same basic ideas. We will, however, stick with axis-aligned elements. This means that collision with rotated elements will not be shown here.

Colliding with tile maps

Finding which tiles of a tile map collide with a sprite can be divided into two parts. First find a box representing the intersection of the two. Then, list all the sprites in this box. A list of some of the possible intersections is shown in red in the following figure:

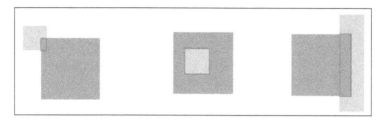

This may at first seem complicated, but it becomes much easier if you consider that it's the exact same problem as finding two one-dimensional intersections (one for each axis).

You may not have realized it, but we used a simplified version of one-dimensional intersections in our *Frogger* clone to detect collisions. The following figure shows what a typical one-dimensional intersection, **i**, of two segments, **a** and **b**, would look like:

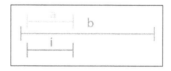

In this situation, the intersection is simply the second element as it's completely contained in the first one. The following figure shows you three other possible situations:

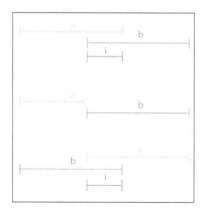

One way to solve the problem is to express the solution from the point of view of the second element. Two points will define the interval; let's call the left-most point i1 and the right-most i2.

Let's first consider the situation where such an intersection really exists, where the two elements are touching. You will probably see that i1 is the bigger point between a1 and b1. In the same manner, i2 is the smaller point between a2 and b2. However, what if the two intervals don't intersect? We will simply return i1=b1 and i2=b1 if the interval a is at its left, and i1=b2 and i2=b2 if the interval a is at its right. To compute this, we just have to constrain the result for i1 and i2 between b1 and b2.

The resulting function would look as follows:

```
gf.intersect = function(a1,a2,b1,b2){
    var i1 = Math.min(Math.max(b1, a1), b2);
    var i2 = Math.max(Math.min(b2, a2), b1);
    return [i1, i2];
}
```

The good part is that we only use two comparisons for each point. Now we can apply this to our two-dimensional problem. The following figure shows you how to decompose the box intersection into two line intersections:

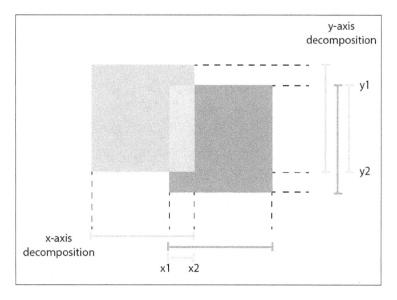

Finding the colliding tiles

Now we will write a function that takes a sprite and a tile map. It will then find the intersections for both axes: x1 to x2 and y1 to y2. Now the point (x1, y1) will be the upper-left corner of the intersection box, and the point (x2, y2) will be the lower-right corner.

However, what we really want for tile maps is not the coordinates but the indexes in the bi-dimensional array. Therefore, we will first transform the coordinate so that the point of origin is the upper-left corner of the tile map. Then, we will divide the new coordinates according to the width and the respective height of a single tile. After rounding the result of this operation, we will have the indexes of the upper-left and lower-right tiles that compose the intersecting box:

```
gf.tilemapBox = function(tilemapOptions, boxOptions){
    var tmX  = tilemapOptions.x;
    var tmXW = tilemapOptions.x + tilemapOptions.width *
tilemapOptions.tileWidth;
    var tmY  = tilemapOptions.y;
    var tmYH = tilemapOptions.y + tilemapOptions.height *
tilemapOptions.tileHeight;

    var bX  = boxOptions.x;
    var bXW = boxOptions.x + boxOptions.width;
    var bY  = boxOptions.y;
    var bYH = boxOptions.y + boxOptions.height;

    var x = gf.intersect(tmX,tmXW, bX, bXW);
    var y = gf.intersect(tmY, tmYH, bY, bYH);

    return {
        x1: Math.floor((x[0] - tilemapOptions.x) / tilemapOptions.
tileWidth),
        y1: Math.floor((y[0] - tilemapOptions.y) / tilemapOptions.
tileHeight),
        x2: Math.ceil((x[1] - tilemapOptions.x) / tilemapOptions.
tileWidth),
        y2: Math.ceil((y[1] - tilemapOptions.y) / tilemapOptions.
tileHeight)
    }
}
```

We will now use this result in the collision detection function. We simply have to list all the tiles between those two points. We will use the bi-dimensional array to find all non-zero entries and then use the classes we defined for the line and column to find our tiles.

```
gf.tilemapCollide = function(tilemap, box){
    var options = tilemap.data("gf");
    var collisionBox = gf.tilemapBox(options, box);
    var divs = []

    for (var i = collisionBox.y1; i < collisionBox.y2; i++){
        for (var j = collisionBox.x1; j < collisionBox.x2; j++){
            var index = options.map[i][j];
            if( index > 0){
                divs.push(tilemap.find(".gf_line_"+i+".gf_
column_"+j));
            }
        }
    }
    return divs;
}
```

This will allow us to find all the tiles colliding with a sprite, but we have to be careful that the coordinate that we give for the sprite and the tile map are correct. If the sprite is in a group that is moved ten pixels to the right, we will have to add ten to the value of the x coordinate of the sprite; otherwise, the collision detection method will not notice it.

We could write a version of this function that looks at the coordinates of all of the sprites and tile maps to find what their relative offset is. This makes the function slightly slower and a bit more complex, but you should be able to do it.

Sprite versus sprite collision

The function to detect whether two sprites collide or not will use the same one-dimensional intersection function we just wrote. To have a collision between the two sprites, we must have a collision on both one-dimensional projections.

If the interval returned by the gf.intersect function has a length of zero (both values are equals), it means that the two sprites collide on this axis. To have a collision between the two sprites, both projections have to collide.

The implementation of our function is very simple as most of the logic is contained in the `gf.intersect` function:

```
gf.spriteCollide = function(sprite1, sprite2){
    var option1 = sprite1.data("gf");
    var option2 = sprite2.data("gf");

    var x = gf.intersect(
        option1.x,
        option1.x + option1.width,
        option2.x,
        option2.x + option2.width);
    var y = gf.intersect(
        option1.y,
        option1.y + option1.height,
        option2.y,
        option2.y + option2.height);

    if (x[0] == x[1] || y[0] == y[1]){
        return false;
    } else {
        return true;
    }
}
```

Coding the game

We now have all the tools we need to start our game. For this game, we will use the wonderful artworks by Kenney Vleugels (http://www.kenney.nl). It will be a classical platformer where the player can move around and jump.

There will be two kinds of enemies, a sort of blob and a flying insect. For the sake of simplicity, the player is immortal and kills the enemies as soon as it touches them. We will describe here each part of the game in the following order:

- Basic setup of the game screen
- Object-oriented code for the player
- Player control
- Parallax scrolling
- Enemies

Basic setup of the game screen

This is very similar to what we did for the *Frogger* clone. Here is how we will organize the game screen:

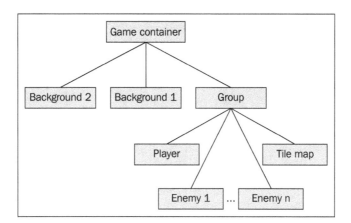

We will have a lot of animations in this game; three for the player, three for each of the two enemies' seven tiles, and two background animations. To make things more readable, we will regroup them. The animations for the player and enemies will each be stored in an object literal, and the animations for the tiles will be stored in an array.

Here is an extract of our code:

```
var playerAnim = {
    stand: new gf.animation({
        url: "player.png",
        offset: 75
    }),
    walk:  new gf.animation({
        url:    "player.png",
        offset: 150,
        width:  75,
        numberOfFrames: 10,
        rate: 90
    }),
    jump:  new gf.animation({
        url: "player.png",
        offset: 900
    })
};
```

```
var slimeAnim = {
    stand: new gf.animation({
        url: "slime.png"
    }),
    walk: new gf.animation({
        url: "slime.png",
        width:  43,
        numberOfFrames: 2,
        rate: 90
    }),
    dead: new gf.animation({
        url: "slime.png",
        offset: 86
    })
};

var flyAnim = {
    stand: new gf.animation({
        url: "fly.png"
    }),
    ...
}
var tiles = [
    new gf.animation({
        url: "tiles.png"
    }),
    new gf.animation({
        url: "tiles.png",
        offset: 70
    }),
    ...
];
```

Object-oriented code for the player

There are many reasons you may want to use object-oriented (OO) code in your game. First, it's a very good way to organize your code. Second, it provides some useful ways to reuse and extend your code.

If you are not familiar with OO programming, JavaScript is probably not the best language to learn. We won't go into the theory of OO; even without it, you should be able to see the logic behind the code we will be writing and what it brings to the table.

As we need only one player, we will create an anonymous class and instantiate it right away. This is quite unusual and only makes sense in this particular situation. Here is the skeleton of our class with all methods, but without their implementation. We will look at each of them later.

```
var player = new (function(){
        var acceleration = 9;
        var speed = 20;
        var status = "stand";
        var horizontalMove = 0;

        this.update = function (delta) {
            //...
        };

        this.left = function (){
            //...
        };

        this.right = function (){
            //...
        };

        this.jump  = function (){
            //...
        };

        this.idle  = function (){
            //...
        };
});
```

As you can see, we begin by defining a few variables that we will use later, and then define the object's methods.

Updating the player's position

We have implemented a very basic physic simulation for player movement along the y axis; if no collision occurs, the avatar will fall with a given acceleration and with a limited maximum speed. This is sufficient to generate neat jump trajectories.

Let's have a look at what the `update` function does. First, it needs to compute the avatar's next position:

```
var delta = 30;
speed = Math.min(100,Math.max(-100,speed + acceleration * delta /
100.0));
var newY = gf.y(this.div) + speed * delta / 100.0;
var newX = gf.x(this.div) + horizontalMove;
var newW = gf.width(this.div);
var newH = gf.height(this.div);
```

You can see in this code that we compute the speed; this is the vertical speed of the player. We use the correct physical rule here, where the speed after a time interval is equal to *the previous speed plus the acceleration time of the interval*. It's then constrained between -100 and 100 to simulate the terminal velocity. Here, the acceleration is constant, as is the gravitational pull.

Then we use this speed to compute the next position along the y axis, again with the correct physical rule.

The new position along the x axis is much simpler; it's the current position modified by the horizontal movement induced by player control (we will see later exactly how this value is generated).

Then we need to check for collision to see if the avatar can really go where it wants or whether there is something on the way. For this, we will use the `gf.tilemapCollision` method we wrote earlier.

Once we have all the tiles that collide with our sprite, what can we do? We will look at any of them and move the sprite out of their way through the shortest possible movement. To do this, we will compute the exact intersection between the sprite and the tile and find whether its width or height is its larger dimension. If the width is more than the height, it means it's a shorter move on the y axis, and if the height is more than the width, it's a shorter move on the x axis.

If we do this for all tiles, we will have moved the avatar to a place where it doesn't collide with any tiles. Here is the full code of what we just described:

```
var collisions = gf.tilemapCollide(tilemap, {x: newX, y: newY, width:
newW, height: newH});
var i = 0;
while (i < collisions.length > 0) {
    var collision = collisions[i];
    i++;
    var collisionBox = {
        x1: gf.x(collision),
```

```
            y1: gf.y(collision),
            x2: gf.x(collision) + gf.width(collision),
            y2: gf.y(collision) + gf.height(collision)
        };

        var x = gf.intersect(newX, newX + newW, collisionBox.
x1,collisionBox.x2);
        var y = gf.intersect(newY, newY + newH, collisionBox.
y1,collisionBox.y2);

        var diffx = (x[0] === newX)? x[0]-x[1] : x[1]-x[0];
        var diffy = (y[0] === newY)? y[0]-y[1] : y[1]-y[0];
        if (Math.abs(diffx) > Math.abs(diffy)){
            // displace along the y axis
             newY -= diffy;
             speed = 0;
             if(status=="jump" && diffy > 0){
                 status="stand";
                 gf.setAnimation(this.div, playerAnim.stand);
             }
        } else {
            // displace along the x axis
            newX -= diffx;
        }
        //collisions = gf.tilemapCollide(tilemap, {x: newX, y: newY,
width: newW, height: newH});
    }
    gf.x(this.div, newX);
    gf.y(this.div, newY);
    horizontalMove = 0;
```

You will notice that if we detect that we need to move the player upward along the y axis, we change the avatar animation and status if the player is jumping. This is simply because this means that the player has landed on the ground.

This code alone is enough to contain all the rules you need to produce a decent movement of the player in the level.

Controlling the player's avatar

All methods except `update` directly correspond to particular types of input from the player. They will be called during the main loop after the corresponding key has been detected as pressed. If no keys are pressed, the idle function will be called.

Let's have a look at the function that moves the player to the left:

```
this.left = function (){
        switch (status) {
            case "stand":
                gf.setAnimation(this.div, playerAnim.walk, true);
                status = "walk";
                horizontalMove -= 7;
                break;
            case "jump":
                horizontalMove -= 5;
                break;
            case "walk":
                horizontalMove -= 7;
                break;
        }
        gf.transform(this.div, {flipH: true});
};
```

Its main part is a switch because we will react differently depending on the state of the player. If the player is currently standing, we will need to change the animation to walking, set the player's new state, and move the player along the x axis. If the player is jumping, we just move the player along the x axis (but slightly slower). If the player is already walking, we just move it.

The last line flips the sprite horizontally because our image depicts the player facing right. The function for the right direction is basically the same.

The `jump` method will check whether the player is currently either standing or walking, and if so, it will change the animations, change the status, and set a vertical speed to generate the jump during the `update` function.

The `idle` status will set the status to standing and the `animation` function accordingly, but only if the player is walking.

```
this.jump  = function (){
    switch (status) {
        case "stand":
        case "walk":
            status = "jump";
            speed = -60;
            gf.setAnimation(this.div, playerAnim.jump);
            break;
    }
};
```

```
this.idle  = function (){
    switch (status) {
        case "walk":
            status = "stand";
            gf.setAnimation(this.div, playerAnim.stand);
            break;
    }
};
```

And that's it for player movement. If you start the game with the logic contained in this object alone, you will already have most of what makes a platformer – a character moving around jumping from one platform to the other.

Player control

We will still need to connect the player's object to the main loop. This is really trivial as all the logic is contained in the object. There is, however, one little detail we omitted. As it is the player will go out of the screen if he moves left. We need to follow him! The way we will implement it is thus: if the player goes beyond a given point, we will start to move the group containing all the sprites and tiles in the opposite direction. This will give the impression that the camera is following the player.

```
var gameLoop = function() {

    var idle = true;
    if(gf.keyboard[37]){ //left arrow
        player.left();
        idle = false;
    }
    if(gf.keyboard[38]){ //up arrow
        player.jump();
        idle = false;
    }
    if(gf.keyboard[39]){ //right arrow
        player.right();
        idle = false;
    }
    if(idle){
        player.idle();
    }

    player.update();
    var margin = 200;
```

```
    var playerPos = gf.x(player.div);
    if(playerPos > 200) {
        gf.x(group, 200 - playerPos);
    }
}
```

This is the main loop containing everything we described earlier.

Parallax scrolling

Parallax scrolling is a very neat way of giving a little depth to a 2D game. It uses the principle that the farther away objects are, the slower they seem to move. It's typically what you see when you look through the side window of a moving car.

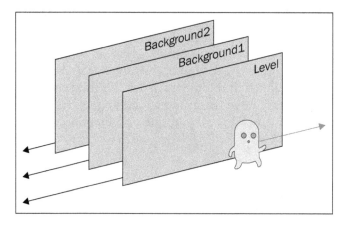

The first layer in the preceding figure will be the group containing all the sprites and the tile map. The second and third layers will simply be images. We will use the same technique we used in the previous game: we will simply use the background position to generate their movement.

The final code takes place in the main game loop just after we move the group around to keep the player visible on screen:

```
var margin = 200;
var playerPos = gf.x(player.div);
if(playerPos > 200) {
    gf.x(group, 200 - playerPos);
    $("#backgroundFront").css("background-position",""+(200 * 0.66 -
playerPos * 0.66)+"px 0px");
    $("#backgroundBack").css("background-position",""+(200 * 0.33 -
playerPos * 0.33)+"px 0px");
}
```

As you can see, the code is simple; the only subtlety is in choosing the right values for the speed of each layer. There is sadly no other way to do this than by observing the effect with the naked eye.

Creating enemies

For the enemies, we will use OO code too. It will allow us to use inheritance only to specify what changes between the two sorts of enemies. The first kind is slime. Enemies of this type crawl on the ground, and when they die, they flatten and stay where they were killed. They patrol back and forth between two points.

The second kind are flies. They behave exactly like the slimes, but they fly in the sky, and once killed, fall into the abyss.

We will start by writing the code for the slimes. It will be similar in structure to the player's object, only much simpler:

```
var Slime = function() {

   this.init = function(div, x1, x2, anim) {
      this.div = div;
      this.x1 = x1;
      this.x2 = x2;
      this.anim = anim;
      this.direction = 1;
      this.speed      = 5;
      this.dead       = false;

      gf.transform(div, {flipH: true});
      gf.setAnimation(div, anim.walk);
   };

   this.update = function(){
      if(this.dead){
         this.dies();
      } else {
         var position = gf.x(this.div);
         if (position < this.x1){
            this.direction = 1;
            gf.transform(this.div, {flipH: true});
         }
         if (position > this.x2){
            this.direction = -1;
            gf.transform(this.div, {flipH: false});
```

```
            }
            gf.x(this.div, gf.x(this.div) + this.direction * this.speed);
        }
    }
    this.kill = function(){
        this.dead = true;
        gf.setAnimation(this.div, this.anim.dead);
    }
    this.dies = function(){}
};
```

Enemies have only two states, alive and dead. It's the `update` function that generates their behavior, either by making them patrol or by letting them die. The only subtlety here is that we use a direction variable to store whether the slime is moving to the left or to the right.

As the behavior of the flies is so similar, we don't need to write much to implement their object:

```
var Fly = function() {}
Fly.prototype = new Slime();
Fly.prototype.dies = function(){
    gf.y(this.div, gf.y(this.div) + 5);
}
```

Here you can see the quite strange syntax for object inheritance in JavaScript (it's called prototypal inheritance). If you're not familiar with it, you should read some advanced books about JavaScript because the full implication of what's going on here is beyond the scope of this book. However, the intuitive way to understand it is this: you create a simple object and copy all the methods of another class into it. Then you modify the classes you want to override.

Here we really just need to change the way the fly behaves after its death by making it fall.

Now we have to call the update function from the main game loop and check for collision with the player. This, again, is done in a very simple way as most of the logic is already written or is in the framework:

```
player.update();
for (var i = 0; i < enemies.length; i++){
    enemies[i].update();
    if (gf.spriteCollide(player.div, enemies[i].div)){
        enemies[i].kill();
    }
}
```

This is it for our game. Of course, like for the last one, there are a lot of things you can add here: give the player the ability to die, allow him to kill enemies only if he jumps on them, or anything you like, really. With this basic template, you'll be able to generate a wide variety of games with vastly different gameplays depending on your choice of the basic rules. Here is what the final game looks like:

Summary

We now know how to draw tile maps and detect collision between them and sprites as well as between sprites. We have a working example of object-oriented code for our game logic that we will be able to use in lots of other kinds of games.

As for our preceding game, the resulting game here can be improved in lots of ways, and I recommend doing so to familiarize yourself even more with the code. You can add more enemies, make them die only if the player jumps on them, and detect when the player reaches the end of the level.

In the next chapter, we will use the techniques we learned here to make a top-view RPG.

5
Putting Things into Perspective

We will now see how to render another very popular kind of effect: the top-down perspective (also known as overhead perspective). There are a wide variety of games that can be created using this technique:

- Hack and slash like *Gauntlet*

- Shoot 'em up like *Alien Breed*

- RPG like *Zelda* or *Chrono Trigger*

- Simulation like *Simcity*

- War game like *Civilization* or *Warcraft*

These games use what is called an orthogonal projection. This can be easily rendered using a simple tile map like the one we implemented in the last chapter. In this chapter, we will make an RPG that will look like *The Legend of Zelda: A Link to the Past* on Super Nintendo.

We will use the graphical assets from BrowserQuest (`http://browserquest.mozilla.org`), a very cool open source game developed by Mozilla to demonstrate the capability of modern browsers. You can see it in the following screenshot:

In this chapter we will cover the following topics:

- Tile map optimization
- Sprite-level occlusion
- Advanced collision detection

At the end of this chapter, we will quickly discuss another variant of the top-down view that can be used for the same kind of games: 2.5D or isometric projection.

Optimizing tile maps for top-down games

The tile map we implemented in the last chapter works well for side scrollers as they typically use a sparse matrix to define their levels. This means that if your level is 100 tiles long and 7 tiles high, it will contain way less than 700 tiles. This allows us to create all those tiles at the beginning of the game.

For a typical top-down game, we find ourselves in a very different situation. Indeed, in order to render the map, all the possible tiles of the tile map used are defined. This means we will have at least 700 tiles for the same level of dimensions. The situation becomes even worse if we use many layers. To reduce this number in order to increase performances, we will have to generate only the tiles that are visible at startup. Then when the view moves, we will have to track which tiles become invisible and delete them, and which tiles become visible and generate them.

There is a tradeoff here; adding and removing tiles will take time, and there is a good chance that it will slow down the game a bit. On the other hand, having a very large amount of tiles in your scene and moving them around will make rendering everything slow.

Ideally, choosing between the two techniques is a matter of testing both and finding which one generates the better result on your target platform. If you really need it, you could even use a hybrid solution where you generate the tile map per chunk. This will allow you to tune when you tolerate the slow down due to the creation and deletion of tiles.

Here we will modify the framework to display only the visible tiles, and this has proven to be fast enough for this kind of game where the player moves at a reasonable speed and where the world is typically quite big.

Finding the visible tiles

The good part is that we already have most of the code we need to find which tiles are visible. Indeed, we have a function that returns the tiles that are colliding with a box. To find the visible tiles, we just need to define this box as the game screen.

```
// find the visible part
var offset = gf.offset(parent);
var visible = gf.tilemapBox(options, {
        x:       -options.x - offset.x,
        y:       -options.x - offset.y,
        width:  gf.baseDiv.width(),
        height: gf.baseDiv.height()
});
```

Here you can see that we use a function to find the offset of the tile map. This is needed because there is the possibility of it being nested into one or more groups that have themselves been moved.

To find the offset, we simply need to look at the current element and all of its parents. We will stop if the parent is not a sprite, group, or tile map. We will also stop if the parent is the base div, that is, the div used to hold the whole game.

```
gf.offset = function(div){
    var options = div.data("gf");
    var x = options.x;
    var y = options.y;

    var parent = $(div.parent());
    options = parent.data("gf");
```

```
      while (!parent.is(gf.baseDiv) && options !== undefined){
          x += options.x;
          y += options.y;
          parent = $(parent.parent());
          options = parent.data("gf");
      }
      return {x: x, y: y};
  }
```

To find if the parent is a group, sprite, or tile map, we check for the presence of an object associated with the key "data".

Except for the part where we find the visible box, the addTilemap function itself hasn't changed much. Here is a short version of it with the changed part highlighted:

```
gf.addTilemap = function(parent, divId, options){
    var options = $.extend({
        x: 0,
        ...
    }, options);

    // find the visible part
    var offset = gf.offset(parent);
    var visible = gf.tilemapBox(options, {
        x:       -options.x - offset.x,
        y:       -options.x - offset.y,
        width:   gf.baseDiv.width(),
        height: gf.baseDiv.height()
    });
      options.visible = visible;

    //create line and row fragment:
    var tilemap = gf.tilemapFragment.clone().attr("id",divId).
data("gf",options);
    for (var i=visible.y1; i < visible.y2; i++){
        for(var j=visible.x1; j < visible.x2; j++) {
            var animationIndex = options.map[i][j];


            ...

        }
    }
    parent.append(tilemap);
    return tilemap;
}
```

Moving the tile map

We now have to track the movement of the tile maps to update which ones are visible. As we have two functions to move any element around, we just have to modify them.

However, we cannot just update tile maps when they are moved around; we also have to update them when any of their parent elements are moved around. jQuery provides a very simple way to find if an element has a tile map as its child or grand child element: .find(). This function searches for any subelement matching the provided selector.

As we add the class gf_tilemap to each of our tile maps, it's very easy to detect them. The following code is the new gf.x function with the change highlighted. The gf.y function is exactly the same.

```
gf.x = function(div,position) {
    if(position !== undefined) {
        div.css("left", position);
        div.data("gf").x = position;

        // if the div is a tile map we need to update the visible part
        if(div.find(".gf_tilemap").size()>0){
            div.find(".gf_tilemap").each(function(){gf.
updateVisibility($(this))});
        }
        if(div.hasClass("gf_tilemap")){
            gf.updateVisibility($(div));
        }
    } else {
        return div.data("gf").x;
    }
}
```

If one of the subelements, or the element itself, is a tile map, we need to update it. We do this with the gf.updateVisibility() function. This function only finds the new visibility box in the tile map and compares it to the old one. This means that we have to keep this visibility stored in the data of the sprite.

The following code is the full implementation of this function:

```
gf.updateVisibility = function(div){
    var options = div.data("gf");
    var oldVisibility = options.visible;
```

```
var parent = div.parent();

var offset = gf.offset(div);
var newVisibility = gf.tilemapBox(options, {
    x:      -offset.x,
    y:      -offset.y,
    width:  gf.baseDiv.width(),
    height: gf.baseDiv.height()
});

if( oldVisibility.x1 !== newVisibility.x1 ||
    oldVisibility.x2 !== newVisibility.x2 ||
    oldVisibility.y1 !== newVisibility.y1 ||
    oldVisibility.y2 !== newVisibility.y2){

    div.detach();

    // remove old tiles
    for(var i = oldVisibility.y1; i < newVisibility.y1; i++){
        for (var j = oldVisibility.x1; j < oldVisibility.x2; j++){
            div.find(".gf_line_"+i+".gf_column_"+j).remove();
        }
    }
    for(var i = newVisibility.y2; i < oldVisibility.y2; i++){
        for (var j = oldVisibility.x1; j < oldVisibility.x2; j++){
            div.find(".gf_line_"+i+".gf_column_"+j).remove();
        }
    }
    for(var j = oldVisibility.x1; j < newVisibility.x1; j++){
        for(var i = oldVisibility.y1; i < oldVisibility.y2; i++){
            div.find(".gf_line_"+i+".gf_column_"+j).remove();
        }
    }
    for(var j = newVisibility.x2; j < oldVisibility.x2; j++){
        for(var i = oldVisibility.y1; i < oldVisibility.y2; i++){
            div.find(".gf_line_"+i+".gf_column_"+j).remove();
        }
    }
    // add new tiles

    for(var i = oldVisibility.y2; i < newVisibility.y2; i++){
        for (var j = oldVisibility.x1; j < oldVisibility.x2; j++){
            createTile(div,i,j,options);
        }
```

```
        }
        for(var i = newVisibility.y1; i < oldVisibility.y1; i++){
            for (var j = oldVisibility.x1; j < oldVisibility.x2; j++){
                createTile(div,i,j,options);
            }
        }
        for(var j = oldVisibility.x2; j < newVisibility.x2; j++){
            for(var i = oldVisibility.y1; i < oldVisibility.y2; i++){
                createTile(div,i,j,options);
            }
        }
        for(var j = newVisibility.x1; j < oldVisibility.x1; j++){
            for(var i = oldVisibility.y1; i < oldVisibility.y2; i++){
                createTile(div,i,j,options);
            }
        }
        div.appendTo(parent);

    }
    // update visibility
    options.visible = newVisibility;
}
```

The first four loops are there to remove the existing tiles that are not visible anymore. Instead of testing whether the tiles to be deleted are on the top or the bottom, we just write two loops. The first one in the code is written as if the tiles to be deleted are on the top. If the tiles to be deleted turn out to be at the bottom as shown in the following figure, the loop won't execute as `oldVisibility.y1 > newVisibility.y1`.

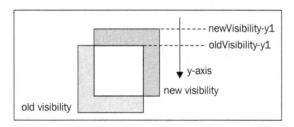

The same goes if the tiles are to be deleted from the top, left, or right. We then use the exact same mechanism to add new tiles. There is, however, one thing we have to be careful about; as we add the tiles horizontally first, when we add them vertically, we have to make sure not to create the tiles we already created a second time. The following figure shows the overlapping tiles:

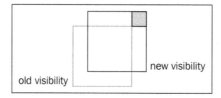

There are more elegant ways to do this, but here we simply check if a tile exists before creating it. This is done in the gf.createTile function.

```
var createTile = function(div, i,j,options){
    var animationIndex = options.map[i][j];
    if(animationIndex > 0 && div.find(".gf_line_"+i+".gf_column_"+j).
size() === 0){
        var tileOptions = {
            x: options.x + j*options.tileWidth,
            y: options.y + i*options.tileHeight,
            width: options.tileWidth,
            height: options.tileHeight
        }
        var tile = gf.spriteFragment.clone().css({
            left:   tileOptions.x,
            top:    tileOptions.y,
            width:  tileOptions.width,
            height: tileOptions.height}
        ).addClass("gf_line_"+i).addClass("gf_column_"+j).data("gf",
tileOptions);

        gf.setAnimation(tile, options.animations[animationIndex-1]);

        div.append(tile);
    }
}
```

With these two changes, the tile maps are now generated dynamically.

Sorting the occlusion

When using top-down views, we will encounter one of the two possibilities: either the "camera" looks straight down at the ground or with a slight angle. The following figure illustrates the two situations:

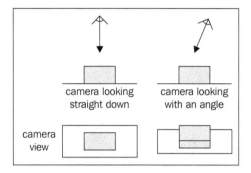

In the first case, the only situation where an element is hidden by another one is if it's straight above it. It's quite easy to produce this effect; we can simply use a group for each altitude and place the sprites and tile maps in the right group.

For example, let's consider a level that contains a tree and a bridge under which the player can walk, just like in the following figure:

We could organize our game screen like this:

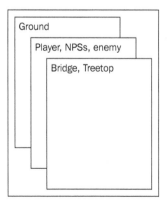

Once this is done, there is not much to worry about. If at some point an NPC (non-player character) or the player moves up or down, we just have to remove them from one group and add them to the other one.

Most modern games, however, use the second type of view, and that's the one we will use for our small game. With this perspective, it's not only the elements above the others but also the ones in front of them that might hide them. The following figure illustrates this:

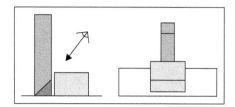

To devise a strictly generic solution for this would be a little overkill for most games and would likely generate some performance issues. Instead, we will use the following tricks to generate a convincing effect.

Sprite occlusion

If we make the following assumptions, the situations for sprites become simple:

- The ground is strictly flat. There may be many flat "floors" with different altitudes but each of them is flat.

- The altitude difference between two flat floors is greater than the size of the biggest NPC or the player.

With these limitations, we can manage sprite occlusion with these two rules:

- If a sprite is on a higher floor than another, the former will always hide the latter

- If two sprites are on the same floor, the one with the bigger y coordinate will always hide the other one

The most straightforward way to implement this is to use the `z-index` CSS property. The implementation would look like this:

```
gf.y(this.div, y);
this.div.css("z-index", y + spriteHeight);
```

Here we need to add the sprite height to the y coordinate because what we need to consider for occlusion is the bottom of the sprite and not the top.

If the sprite is one floor higher, we will add to make sure that its z index is bigger than all the sprites in the floor above. Let's say we give an index to each level, 0 being the lowest one, 1 the one above, and so on; in this case, the formula to generate the z index from the y coordinate would be:

```
z-index = y-coordinate + spriteHeight + floorIndex * floorHeight
```

In our game, all of our sprites will be on the same level so we won't need to use this function, and we could stick with the preceding code.

Level versus sprite occlusion

If we stick to the same assumption as before, we don't need to do much to generate an occlusion of sprites from the background. Our level is defined using tile maps. When designing the level, we will separate our tiles into two tile maps: one being the floor and the other one being everything above it.

For example, let's consider a scene with a tree and a house:

We will store the ground, the bottom of the house, and the trunk of the tree in one tile map, and we will store the top of the house as well as the foliage of the tree in another one.

Collision detection

Collision detection is slightly different for this game as for the previous one. As we use collision instead of per-pixel collision with the sprite-bounding box, we find ourselves in a situation where we might detect a collision where only the sprites' non-transparent pixels are colliding, as shown in the following figure:

However, there is a very easy solution to this problem without resorting to per-pixel or polygonal collision detection; we will use a second transparent sprite to create the zone we really want to use for collision detection.

Player versus environment collisions

In our game, we will use a technique often used in RPG; the player avatar will be made of not only one sprite but of a superposition of sprites. This will allow us to change the armor the avatar wears, change the weapon he uses, his haircut, skin color, and so on, without having to generate all the possible combinations of those variants.

In our game, we will only use two images for the player avatar: the player and its weapon. We will place them into a group; this will make it easy to move them around.

To these two sprites, we will first add a transparent sprite that will define the collision zone for the collision with the environment. The following figure shows exactly that:

As you can see, we've chosen a collision box that is as wide as the body of the player avatar, but slightly shorter. This is to account for the situation where the player approaches an obstacle from below. As shown in the previous figure, his head will hide a part of the bottom of this object. With this smaller collision box, we automatically generate this effect.

Now we don't want the avatar to collide with every element of the level. For example, it shouldn't collide with the ground or with anything above it.

If you remember, we separated the level into two tile maps before. To make collision detection easier, we will simply separate the lower one in two as well:

- One containing all the ground elements that don't collide with the player
- One containing all the elements that collide with the player

This means that we now have three tile maps for the level.

As you can imagine, designing this level and adding all the tiles to the right tile map is becoming too complicated as we write all the arrays by hand. Instead, we will use a tile map editor.

Using a tile map editor

There are quite a few free and open source tile map editors around. For this game, we will use Tiled (`http://www.mapeditor.org/`). It has the advantage that it allows the tile maps to be exported to a JSON file.

The images that we will use to create our level come from the game BrowserQuest by Mozilla. The following figure shows a part of it:

As you can see, we have tiles for grassy ground, tiles for sandy ground, and tiles that represent the transition to sandy ground. The transition tiles are half transparent and half sandy. This allows us to transit to sandy ground from any other type of ground.

This means we will have to use yet another tile map. The lower tile map will be divided in two: one with all the ground elements and one with the transition elements that contain transparent pixels and don't collide with the player. However, in total we will have four tile maps to draw our level. For example, a part of our level with sand, grass, and a tree would look like this:

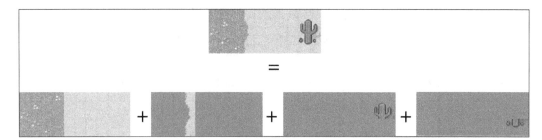

We won't look at the entire code that imports the JSON file generated by Tiled. If you want more details, just look at the gf.importTiled function. The important part is that we use jQuery's $.ajax function. With this function, we will be able to load the JSON file. The trick is to use the right parameter to call it:

```
$.ajax({
    url: url,
    async: false,
    dataType: 'json',
    success: function(json){...}
);
```

jQuery also provides a shorthand function called `$.getJSON`, but we want to have a synchronous call and that's only possible with `$.ajax`. With these calls, the function we provided to the success parameter will be called once the JSON file is loaded. It's in this function that we will import the file.

If you want to see exactly how we do it, you can simply look at the provided code for this chapter.

Now that we are using the `$.ajax` function, we just have to make sure that we access our code from a server to test it as simply opening our HTML file in a browser won't work anymore. If you don't have a server running, you can use EasyPHP on Windows (`http://www.easyphp.org`), or MAMP on OS X (`http://www.mamp.info`).

Player versus sprite collision

We will only support one kind of sprite versus sprite collision detection here: the player attacking an enemy or talking to an NPC. Like before, we will need a transparent sprite to define the zone where the collision should be detected. Except this time, this zone is not on the player itself but in front of him, as shown in the following screenshot:

The only trick is that this zone has to be moved around to always face the direction where the player is looking. If we take the same OO code that we used for the last game to implement the player, it would look something like this:

```
var player = new (function(){
    // the group holding both the player sprite and the weapon
    this.div = $();
    // the sprite holding the player's avatar
    this.avatar = $();
    // the sprite holding the weapon
    this.weapon = $();
    // the hit zone
    this.hitzone  = $();
```

```
// collision zone
this.colzone = $();

//...

this.update = function () {
    //...
};

this.left = function (){
    if(state !== "strike"){
        if(orientation !== "left" && moveY === 0 && moveX === 0){
            orientation = "left";
            gf.x(this.hitzone, 16);
            gf.y(this.hitzone, 16);
            gf.h(this.hitzone,  128 + 32);
            gf.w(this.hitzone, 64);
            //...

        }
        //...
    }
};

this.right = function (){
    //...
};

this.up = function (){
    //...
};

this.down = function (){
    if(state !== "strike"){
        if(orientation !== "down" && moveY === 0 && moveX === 0) {
            orientation = "down";
            state = "walk";
            gf.x(this.hitzone, 16);
            gf.y(this.hitzone, 192-80);
            gf.w(this.hitzone,  128 + 32);
            gf.h(this.hitzone, 64);
            //...
        }
```

```
            //...
        }
    };

    //...
});
```

The highlighted parts of the code show where we change the position of the collision zone for interaction with NPCs and enemies. We call this the sprite hit zone because it represents the zone that is covered by a swing of the player's sword.

To choose the right size and position for this hit zone, you really have to fine-tune it to the images you use.

In the main game loop, we will then check for collision between this zone and a list of NPCs and then enemies.

```
this.detectInteraction = function(npcs, enemies, console){
    if(state == "strike" && !interacted){
        for (var i = 0; i < npcs.length; i++){
            if(gf.spriteCollide(this.hitzone, npcs[i].div)){
                npcs[i].object.dialog();
                interacted = true;
                return;
            }
        }
        for (var i = 0; i < enemies.length; i++){
            if(gf.spriteCollide(this.hitzone, enemies[i].div)){
                // handle combat
                interacted = true;
                return;
            }
        }
    }
};
```

Talking to NPCs

The only interaction we will implement with NPCs is a one-way dialog. When the player hits an NPC, we will display a line of dialog. If he hits it again and the NPC has more to say, we will display the next line of dialog.

We will use a line at the bottom of the screen to display this text. This line has to be semitransparent to let the player see the level behind it, and it has to be over all the elements of the game. This is how we will create it:

```
container.append("<div id='console' style='font-family: \"Press Start
2P\", cursive; color: #fff; width: 770px; height: 20px; padding: 15px;
position: absolute; bottom: 0; background: rgba(0,0,0,0.5); z-index:
3000'>");
```

This type of interface is typically called a console. To make it semitransparent and still leave the text inside it opaque, we apply a transparent background color by calling the `rgba()` function. To make sure it floats over all the game elements, we give it a big enough z index.

To display text in this console, we simply have to use `.html()`. The following code is the complete implementation of the NPCs:

```
var NPC = function(name, text, console){
    var current = 0;

    this.getText = function(){
        if(current === text.length){
            current = 0;
            return "[end]";
        }
        return name + ": " + text[current++];
    };

    this.dialog = function(){
        console.html(this.getText());
    }
}
```

And this is how we will instantiate one of them:

```
npcs.push({
    div: gf.addSprite(npcsGroup,"NPC1", {
        x:      800,
        y:      800,
        width:  96,
        height: 96
    }),
    object: new NPC("Dr. Where", ["Welcome to this small
universe...","I hope you will enjoy it.","You should head east from
here...","there's someone you may want to meet."], console)
});
```

```
npcs[npcs.length-1].object.div = npcs[npcs.length-1].div;
gf.setAnimation(npcs[npcs.length-1].div, new gf.animation({
    url: "npc/scientist.png"
}));
$("#NPC1").css("z-index",800 + 96);
```

Nothing very special here; we just have to make sure to set the correct z index too.

Fighting enemies

To fight enemies, we will simulate the throw of a dice. The rule of combat is quite typical in an RPG: the player throws a dice to the player and adds it to a fixed value called the attack modifier. This will generate the attack value of the player's strike. The enemy will try to defend itself by throwing a dice to the enemy and add it to its own defense modifier.

If the player's strike is bigger than the enemy's defense, the attack is successful and the enemy will suffer a loss of life equal to the player's strike. If the enemy's defense is stronger, the attack fails and the enemy remains safe.

The following code is the implementation of this mechanism:

```
if(gf.spriteCollide(this.hitzone, enemies[i].div)){
    var enemyRoll = enemies[i].object.defend();
    var playerRoll = Math.round(Math.random() * 6) + 5;

    if(enemyRoll <= playerRoll){
        var dead = enemies[i].object.kill(playerRoll);
        console.html("You hit the enemy "+playerRoll+"pt");
        if (dead) {
            console.html("You killed the enemy!");
            enemies[i].div.fadeOut(2000, function(){
                $(this).remove();
            });
            enemies.splice(i,1);
        }
    } else {
        console.html("The enemy countered your attack");
    }
    interacted = true;
    return;
}
```

Here we use the console to display the progress of the combat to the player. The formula for the combat could be different depending on additional parameters, such as the bonus provided by the weapon the player uses and the enemy's armor. It's really up to you to find out what you want to consider when deciding if a strike is successful.

We didn't implement this, but the enemy striking back would be exactly the same.

The complete game

That's it for this game. All the rest of the implementation is taken straight from the game we created in *Chapter 4, Looking Sideways*. We use the same object-oriented code of the player and the other sprites to resolve the collision between the player and the level.

A good exercise would be to make the enemies move around and attack the player, implement an experience and life bar for the player, and design a bigger world and more NPCs to make the story more interesting. Indeed, that's what makes RPGs so great to write; they are a great medium for telling stories!

Another way you could improve this game is to use an isometric projection instead of an orthogonal one. Explaining how to write a general-purpose isometric engine is outside the scope of this book, but if you want to learn more about this, you could read *Making Isometric Social Real-Time Games with HTML5, CSS3, and JavaScript* by *Andres Pagella* (http://shop.oreilly.com/product/0636920020011.do).

Isometric tiles

There are two difficulties when dealing with isometric tiles. First, it's very simple to display an orthogonal grid with DOM elements, whereas it's more complicated to display an isometric one. Secondly, the occlusion is harder to compute.

Drawing an isometric tile map

We will use a trick here to generate our tile map. Each of our tiles will be stored in an area where they are surrounded by transparent pixels in such a way as to give them a square shape, just like the following screenshot:

To make the magic happen, we will use two normal tile maps to display one isometric one. They will overlap, but with an offset between them equal to half the height and half the width of one tile. The following figure shows you how it would look:

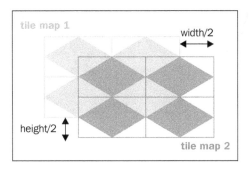

Occlusion for isometric games

The occlusion for isometric games is harder to manage than for orthogonal ones. In this situation, you can't simply play with layers to generate the correct occlusion. Instead, you will have to give a z index to each "block" positioned in the level (such as the walls, trees, objects, and others).

The value of this occlusion will depend on its coordinate just as in the case of the player, NPCs, and enemies previously. This means that you will need to post-process the tile map and generate them. This process can be quite complex to automate, and if the number of elements in your game is reasonably small, you may want to do it by hand. Otherwise, you will need to have some sort of 3D model of where each block belongs.

Summary

In this chapter, you have learned how to use tile maps to their full potential. You can now write a wide variety of games using the techniques you have learned in this chapter and the previous one. You will probably find out that the problems you encounter while writing a game are often the same. The best solution, however, often depends on your game's limitations and constraints.

When you start writing your game, don't try to implement a general solution but instead first focus on your particular situation. The result will most likely be faster, easier to maintain, and will take you less time to implement.

In the next chapter, we will learn how to implement a multilevel game using the platformer we created in *Chapter 4, Looking Sideways*.

6
Adding Levels to Your Games

Until now all of our games have had only one level. This is nice for a demo or a proof of concept, but you probably want to have many levels in your game. As always there are many ways to do this, but most of them are based on the idea that each of your levels are described by their own file (or files).

We will begin this chapter by quickly exploring the different ways to combine files to create your game. We will then look at the jQuery functions that allow such techniques.

Finally, we will take the game we developed in *Chapter 4*, *Looking Sideways*, and extend it to include three levels by implementing some of the techniques described beforehand.

The following is a quick list of the topics we will cover in this chapter:

- Using multiple files for your game
- Loading files with `$.ajax`
- Executing remote JavaScript
- Adding a new level to our game

Implementing a multi-file game

The first thing you have to ask yourself is, "When are the other files loaded?" The classical approach is to have simple levels and load the next one at the end of the previous one. This is the typical scenario for a platform game.

Another approach is to have one big level and load a sublevel when you reach a given point. Typically, in an RPG the big level would be the outside world and the sublevel would be the inside of buildings. In both of these examples, the loading of the file doesn't need to be done asynchronously.

The last common approach is to have a single very large level made of many sublevels. This is typically what you have for MMORPG. Here you need to load the files asynchronously so that the player doesn't notice that the sublevel has to be loaded.

The challenge you will face depends greatly on which of the aforementioned situations you find yourself in. They can be divided as follows: loading a tile map, a sprite, and loading a logic behavior.

Loading tile maps

If you remember, in *Chapter 5, Putting Things into Perspective*, we loaded the tile map in the form of a JSON file. As we explained earlier, we load a JSON file that holds the description of the tile map. To do this, we use the basic AJAX function in jQuery: `$.ajax()`. We will later see all the details about using this function.

However, simply loading a tile map is often not enough to describe your level entirely. You may want to specify where the end of the level is, what are the areas that will kill the player, and so on. One common technique is to use a secondary tile map, one that is invisible and holds tiles that adds meaning to the other tile map.

The following figure shows an example of this:

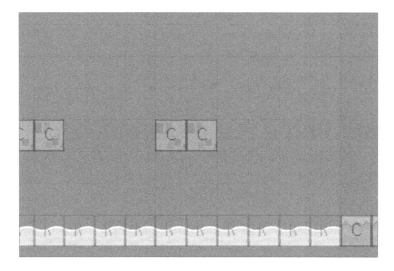

This has several advantages:

- You can easily give the same semantic meaning to different tiles. For example, tiles with or without grass can represent the ground and interact in the exact same way with the player.

- You can give the same semantic meaning to tiles of two levels that use completely different tile sets. This way you don't really have to worry about what images are used in your levels as long as they use the same logic tiles to model it.

Implementing this isn't really hard. The following code shows the changes in the `gf.addTilemap` function:

```
gf.addTilemap = function(parent, divId, options){
    var options = $.extend({
        x: 0,
        y: 0,
        tileWidth: 64,
        tileHeight: 64,
        width: 0,
        height: 0,
        map: [],
        animations: [],
        logic: false
    }, options);

    var tilemap = gf.tilemapFragment.clone().attr("id",divId).
data("gf",options);

    if (!options.logic){

        // find the visible part
        var offset = gf.offset(parent);
        var visible = gf.tilemapBox(options, {
            x:      -options.x - offset.x,
            y:      -options.x - offset.y,
            width:  gf.baseDiv.width(),
            height: gf.baseDiv.height()
        });
        options.visible = visible;

        //create line and row fragment:
        for (var i=visible.y1; i < visible.y2; i++){
            for(var j=visible.x1; j < visible.x2; j++) {
```

```
                    var animationIndex = options.map[i][j];

                if(animationIndex > 0){
                    var tileOptions = {
                        x: options.x + j*options.tileWidth,
                        y: options.y + i*options.tileHeight,
                        width: options.tileWidth,
                        height: options.tileHeight
                    }
                    var tile = gf.spriteFragment.clone().css({
                        left:   tileOptions.x,
                        top:    tileOptions.y,
                        width:  tileOptions.width,
                        height: tileOptions.height}
                    ).addClass("gf_line_"+i).addClass("gf_column_"+j).
data("gf", tileOptions);

                    gf.setAnimation(tile, options.
animations[animationIndex-1]);

                    tilemap.append(tile);
                }
            }
        }
    }
    parent.append(tilemap);
    return tilemap;
}
```

As you can see, we simply add a flag to indicate if the tile maps are here for a logical purpose. If so, we don't need to create any tiles in it.

The collision detection function is now slightly modified too. In the case of a logical tile map we can't simply return the divs. Instead, we will return an object literal containing the size, position, and type of the colliding tiles. The following code extract shows exactly this:

```
gf.tilemapCollide = function(tilemap, box){
    var options = tilemap.data("gf");
    var collisionBox = gf.tilemapBox(options, box);
    var divs = []

    for (var i = collisionBox.y1; i < collisionBox.y2; i++){
        for (var j = collisionBox.x1; j < collisionBox.x2; j++){
            var index = options.map[i][j];
```

```
        if( index > 0){
            if(options.logic) {
            divs.push({
                    type:    index,
                    x:       j*options.tileWidth,
                    y:       i*options.tileHeight,
                    width:   options.tileWidth,
                    height:  options.tileHeight
            });
            } else {
                    divs.push(tilemap.find(".gf_line_"+i+".gf_
column_"+j));
            }
            }
        }
    }
    return divs;
}
```

Once this feature is implemented, it becomes very easy to load the level. Indeed, as long as the logical tile map is present and the game's code knows how to react to each tile, we don't need anything more to make the player react to its environment.

Loading sprites and their behavior

If loading a tile map from a different file is pretty straightforward, there are plenty of ways to do the same for the sprites that a level contains.

You can implement an interpreter for a JSON file that will in turn create and configure the enemies and NPCs. This has the advantage that you could merge this JSON and the one describing the tile map. This way you would only need to load one file instead of two. As there's a pretty big overhead for each file you load, the size of the file has little impact; in most situations it will make your level load faster. The following diagram illustrates this:

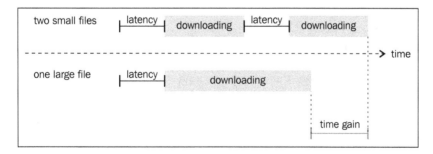

It has some disadvantages too: first your engine has to be written to understand every possible behavior you may want your enemies to adopt. It means that if you have a kind of enemy that is used only once in the tenth level of the game, you will still need to load its implementation at the same time you load the game at startup. If you work in a team and the other members want to implement their own type of enemy, they will need to modify the engine instead of just working on their level.

You will also need to be really careful to specify a JSON format that covers all your needs or you run the risk of having to refactor a big part of your game later on. The following code is an example of how such a JSON file might look like the following code:

```json
{
    "enemies" : [
        {
            "name" : "Monster1",
            "type" : "spider",
            "positionx" : 213,
            "positiony" : 11,
            "pathx" : [250,300,213],
            "pathy" : [30,11,11]
        },
        {
            "name" : "Monster2",
            "type" : "fly",
            "positionx" : 345,
            "positiony" : 100,
            "pathx" : [12,345],
            "pathy" : [100,100]
        }
    ],
    "npcs" : [
        {
            "name" : "Johny",
            "type" : "farmer",
            "positionx" : 202,
            "positiony" : 104,
            "dialog" : [
                "Hi, welcome to my home,",
                "Feel free to wander around!"
            ]
        }
    ]
}
```

Another possible implementation is to load a complete script that will in turn create the enemies and configure them. This has the advantage of making your game more modular and loosening the coupling between the game and the levels.

It has several disadvantages though. First, if you're not careful, the code of your level has the potential to override some of your main game variables. This will create bugs that are quite difficult to track and will depend on the order the levels have been loaded. Secondly, you will have to be extra careful with choosing your variable scope as each newly loaded level's code is executed in the global scope.

In the example given in this chapter, we will choose the second solution because it makes sense for a small game and is quite flexible.

No matter which of those you choose to implement, you will most likely use $.ajax or one of its aliases. In the next section, we will take a detailed look at it.

Using $.ajax

The $.ajax function is a very powerful, but low-level function. It has many aliases that can be used for different specific tasks:

- $.get is a multi-purpose alias that reduces the number of options in comparison with $.ajax and has an API based on multiple optional parameters instead of a single object literal. It always loads files asynchronously.

- $.getJSON is a function used to load a JSON file asynchronously.

- $.getScript is a function that loads a script asynchronously and then executes it.

- $.load is a function that loads an HTML file asynchronously and injects its content in the selected element.

- $.post is similar to $.get, but uses a post request.

As you can see all these aliases have one thing in common: they all load their files asynchronously. This means that if you rather load your resource synchronously, you are back to using $.ajax. However, be reassured it's not really more complicated than the aliases once you know the right parameters. Furthermore, the API documentation for the aliases always include the exact parameter to use for an $.ajax call to have the same effect.

When using $.ajax, you have to make sure that you access the files through a server and that you respect the same-origin policy. Otherwise, you will likely run into problems on most browsers. To learn more about $.ajax you should look at the official jQuery API documentation (http://api.jquery.com/jQuery.ajax/).

Loading a JSON file

JSON files are a very convenient way to load external data without having to parse it yourself. Once loaded, a JSON file is typically stored in a simple JavaScript object. Then you can simply look up its properties to access the data.

If you want to mimic a call to `$.getJSON` with `$.ajax` it will look something like the following code:

```
$.ajax({
  url: url,
  dataType: 'json',
  data: data,
  success: callback
});
```

Here, `url` is the web address of the JSON file, `data` is an optional list of parameters you may want to pass to the server, and `success` is the callback that will handle the JSON file once it's loaded. If you want to access the remote file synchronously, you have to add the parameter `async : false` to the call.

It's in the callback that you will decide what to do with the JSON file; it will have the following signature:

```
var callback = success(data, textStatus, jqXHR)
```

Here, `data` holds the object generated from the JSON file. What you will do with it really depends on your use case; here is a short version of the code that imports the tile maps generated by Tiled:

```
success: function(json){
  //...

  var layers = json.layers;
  var usedTiles = [];
  var animationCounter = 0;
  var tilemapArrays = [];

  // Detect which animations we need to generate
  // and convert the tiles array indexes to the new ones
  for (var i=0; i < layers.length; i++){
    if(layers[i].type === "tilelayer"){
      // ...
      tilemapArrays.push(tilemapArray);
    }
  }
```

```
        // adding the tilemaps
        for (var i=0; i<tilemapArrays.length; i++){
            tilemaps.push(gf.addTilemap(parent, divIdPrefix+i, {
                x:          0,
                y:          0,
                tileWidth:  tileWidth,
                tileHeight: tileHeight,
                width:      width,
                height:     height,
                map:        tilemapArrays[i],
                animations: animations,
                logic: (layers[i].name === "logic")
                }));
        }
    }
});
```

The highlighted part is quite typical. Indeed, most non-trivial JSON will hold
an array of elements to make it possible to describe any number of similar entities.
When you are not the designer of the JSON file specification, you may find yourself
in the situation where you have to convert the content of the JSON object to your
own data structure. That's exactly what this code does.

There is no general approach here and you really have to consider each situation
individually. The nice thing is that in most cases this piece of code is executed
only a few times during the game and therefore, is not sensible with regard to
performances. You're better off making it as readable as possible rather than
searching all the places where you can make it run faster.

Loading a remote script

If you want to mimic the usage of $.getScript with $.ajax, it will look something
like the following:

```
$.ajax({
  url: url,
  dataType: "script",
  success: success
});
```

As we did earlier, you can make it synchronous simply by adding async : false
to the list of parameters. This will do two things: load the script and execute it. The
callback is not that important here, it will only allow you to track whether the file
was successfully retrieved or not.

As mentioned earlier, the script will be executed in the global scope. This has some implication on your code organization. Until now the code of our games looked like the following:

```
$(function() {
    var someVariable = "someValue";

    var someFunction = function(){
        //do something
    }
});
```

Here all the functions and variables are defined in a "private" scope that cannot be touched from outside. This means that if your remote code tries to do something like the following, it will fail:

```
var myVariable = someVariable;
someFunction();
```

Indeed, the functions `someFunction` and `someVariable` are not visible from the global scope. The solution is to carefully choose which variable and function should be visible from the remote code and put them in the global scope. In our situation it might look like the following:

```
var someVariable = "someValue";
var someFunction = function(){
    //do something
}

$(function() {
    // do something else
});
```

You may want to keep all these in a namespace like we did for our framework. As you're writing a final product that won't likely be used as a library in another, it has more to do with personal preference.

Debugging calls to $.ajax

Now that we are loading remote files, a new variety of problems can occur: the URL of the file may no longer be valid, the server may be down, or the file may be ill formatted. In production, you may want to detect these at runtime to display a message to the user instead of simply crashing. During the development phase, you may want to find out exactly what went wrong in order to debug your code.

jQuery provides three functions that you can use to perform this: .done(), .fail(), and .always(). There used to be three others (.success(), .error(), and .complete()), but they have been deprecated since jQuery 1.8.

.done()

.done() can be used instead of the success callback. It will only be called once the file is successfully loaded. The provided function will be called with the following three arguments in this order: data, textStatus, jqXHR.

data is the loaded file, which means you could handle your JSON file there if you wanted to.

.fail()

.fail() is called whenever a problem occurred. The provided function will be called with the following three arguments in this order: jqXHR, textStatus, exception.

When loading and executing a script, it's very convenient to find what happened if the script is not executed. Indeed, the exceptions won't appear in most browsers' debug consoles, but the exception argument will contain the exact exception thrown by your code.

For example, if we look at the scope problem described earlier where the main game contains the following code:

```
$(function() {
    var someVariable = "someValue";

    var someFunction = function(){
        //do something
    }
});
```

And a remote script like this:

```
someFunction();
```

You could catch the exception by writing:

```
$.getScript("myScript.js").fail(function(jqxhr, textStatus, exception)
{
    console.log("Error: "+exception);
});
```

And the following error would be written to the console:

```
error: ReferenceError: someFunction is not defined
```

This will work to detect other problems such as unresponsive servers and so on.

Modifying our platform game

We now have all the knowledge we need for creating a multi-level game. First, we will create a list of levels and a function to load them:

```
var levels = [
        {tiles: "level1.json", enemies: "level1.js"},
        {tiles: "level2.json", enemies: "level2.js"}
    ];

var currentLevel = 0;

var loadNextLevel = function(group){
    var level = levels[currentLevel++];
    // clear old level
    $("#level0").remove();
    $("#level1").remove();
    for(var i = 0; i < enemies.length; i++){
        enemies[i].div.remove();
    }
    enemies = [];

    // create the new level

    // first the tiles
    gf.importTiled(level.tiles, group, "level");

    // then the enemies
    $.getScript(level.enemies);

    // finaly return the div holdoing the tilemap
    return $("#level1");
}
```

The highlighted lines are the ones that do the remote loading of files. This uses the functions described earlier. As you can see, there is no mechanism to detect that the game is over. You could add one as homework if you want to!

Before the next level is loaded, we have to make sure to delete the existing one as well as the enemies it contains.

Now we will change the game to work with logic tiles instead of standard ones. This way we can have a kind of tile that defines the end of one level. Here is our collision detection code modified to do exactly that:

```
var collisions = gf.tilemapCollide(tilemap, {x: newX, y: newY, width:
newW, height: newH});
var i = 0;
while (i < collisions.length > 0) {
    var collision = collisions[i];
    i++;
    var collisionBox = {
        x1: collision.x,
        y1: collision.y,
        x2: collision.x + collision.width,
        y2: collision.y + collision.height
    };

    // react differently to each kind of tile
    switch (collision.type) {
        case 1:
            // collision tiles
            var x = gf.intersect(newX, newX + newW, collisionBox.
x1,collisionBox.x2);
            var y = gf.intersect(newY, newY + newH, collisionBox.
y1,collisionBox.y2);

            var diffx = (x[0] === newX)? x[0]-x[1] : x[1]-x[0];
            var diffy = (y[0] === newY)? y[0]-y[1] : y[1]-y[0];
            if (Math.abs(diffx) > Math.abs(diffy)){
                // displace along the y axis
                newY -= diffy;
                speed = 0;
                if(status=="jump" && diffy > 0){
                    status="stand";
                    gf.setAnimation(this.div, playerAnim.stand);
                }
            } else {
                // displace along the x axis
                newX -= diffx;
            }
            break;
        case 2:
            // deadly tiles
            // collision tiles
```

```
            var y = gf.intersect(newY, newY + newH, collisionBox.
y1,collisionBox.y2);
                var diffy = (y[0] === newY)? y[0]-y[1] : y[1]-y[0];
                if(diffy > 40){
                    status = "dead";
                }
                break;
            case 3:
                // end of level tiles
                status = "finished";
                break;
        }


    }
```

As you can see, we've added the possibility for the player to die when he/she hits some tiles. This will make him/her reappear at the beginning of the current level. If the tiles are of type 3, we set the status of the player as finished. Later, we detect the status and load the next level.

```
if (status == "finished") {
    tilemap             = loadNextLevel(group);
    gf.x(this.div, 0);
    gf.y(this.div, 0);
    status = "stand";
    gf.setAnimation(this.div, playerAnim.jump);
}
```

Don't forget to rest the player position too, otherwise, it will appear in the middle of the next level instead of at its starting point.

We now have to write each script that creates the enemies for their respective level. This is almost the exact same piece of code that we used in the previous version of the game, but placed in a separate file:

```
var group = $("#group");

var fly1   = new Fly();
fly1.init(
    gf.addSprite(group,"fly1",{width: 69, height: 31, x: 280, y:
220}),
    280, 490,
    flyAnim
);
enemies.push(fly1);
```

```
var slime1 = new Slime();
slime1.init(
    gf.addSprite(group,"slime1",{width: 43, height: 28, x: 980, y:
392}),
    980, 1140,
    slimeAnim
);
enemies.push(slime1);

var slime2 = new Slime();
slime2.init(
    gf.addSprite(group,"slime2",{width: 43, height: 28, x: 2800, y:
392}),
    2800, 3000,
    slimeAnim
);
enemies.push(slime2);
```

As you may already have figured, we cannot simply run the game and use that script without modifying our code some more. As we said before, the remote script will be executed in the global scope and we need to move the pieces it uses to it.

Here we need the enemies' objects and animations as well as the array that contains the list of enemies. We will simply take those out of their closure and add them at the beginning of our game script:

```
var enemies = [];
var slimeAnim = {
    stand: new gf.animation({
        url: "slime.png"
    }),
    // ...

}
var flyAnim = {
    stand: new gf.animation({
        url: "fly.png"
    }),
    // ...}

var Slime = function() {
    // ...
};
var Fly = function() {}
Fly.prototype = new Slime();
```

```
Fly.prototype.dies = function(){
    gf.y(this.div, gf.y(this.div) + 5);
}

$(function() {
    // here come the rest of the game
});
```

Now the game will contain as many levels as we want. Have fun with the level editor! Here we used the scripts only to set the enemies, but we could use it to change the level background if we wanted to.

Summary

Making your game multileveled adds a few new tricks to your sleeve. Now you've learned to divide your assets in many files and load them when you need them. You've also learned how to use tiles to describe logic behavior and not only the graphical aspect of your levels.

As mentioned earlier, there is much more that can be done with the game to make it really fun. I will recommend spending quite some time on level design. In most commercial games, this is where most of the time is spent, so don't hesitate to stop coding for a while and start making and testing your levels!

In the next chapter, you will learn how to make a multiplayer game. For this we will use the game we created in *Chapter 5, Putting Things into Perspective*, and add new functionality to it in the same way we did for the game from *Chapter 4, Looking Sideways*, which we used in this chapter.

7
Making a Multiplayer Game

Single player games are fun, and as we've already seen, there is a large variety of them you can make with JavaScript. However, having your game run in a web browser, there is a huge temptation to make it multiplayer. This is exactly what we will do in this chapter and what better example of a multiplayer game than an MMORPG!

We will take our small single-player RPG from *Chapter 5*, *Putting Things into Perspective*, and transform it into a brand new MMORPG: *World of Ar'PiGi*.

However, first a word of warning—the technology we will use to implement the server-side of our game is PHP + MySQL. The reason for this is it's by far the most common technology around. If you have some sort of hosting, chances are it's supported out of the box.

There are many reasons why this is not necessarily the best solution. When writing a game where the server-side usage is not reduced to simply serving a static page, you have to think very carefully about scaling:

- How many users will be able to play simultaneously on your system?
- What will you do when the number of players grows past this limit?
- How much are you ready to pay to make your server run?
- What is the quality of service you want to provide to the player?

The answer to these questions should dictate what technology and infrastructure you will choose. It is not the purpose of this book to elaborate on this; the solution we will implement should scale up to a few tens of players without any problems, but the techniques you will learn here can be applied no matter what software solution or hosting you choose!

In this chapter, we will cover the following subjects:

- Multiplayer game specification
- Managing a player's account
- Synchronizing a player's state
- Managing the enemies' server-side

World of Ar'PiGi

The game we will create based on our previous RPG will have the following features:

- A player can create an account and log into the game with it
- When they come back to the game, their avatar will reappear where it was when they left
- Each player can see all the other players that are playing at the same time
- The name of the other players will appear above their avatar
- The state of the enemies is managed server side: if someone kills a monster, it will be dead for all the other players as well

This game will have some of the same limitations of the game it's based on. The monster won't fight back and won't move around.

Managing the player's account

Let's start with the basics: let the player create an account and log into the game. To store information server side, we will use a database (MySQL). The table structure we will use is very simple as there is not much to store. The player's account will be stored in a table we will creatively call `players`.

This table will have the following rows:

- NAME: This is a string holding the name of the player. It will be unique so that no two players can have the same name.
- PW: This is a string holding the player's password. It is hashed (more on this in the next section, *Searching elements in the database*).
- X: This is a double that will hold the player's x coordinate.
- Y: This is a double that will hold the player's y coordinate.
- DIR: This is an integer that we will use to store the direction the player is facing.

- STATE: This is an integer that holds the state of the player: standing, walking, or fighting.
- LASTUPDATE: This is a time stamp that will hold the last time the server heard from the player.

A SQL script is provided that creates all the tables you need for the game in the file `create_tables.sql`.

To create the user interface that allows creating an account or logging into the game, we will use a series of divs that will overlap the game screen. Only one of them will be visible at any time. The following figure shows the possible user interactions and the corresponding screens:

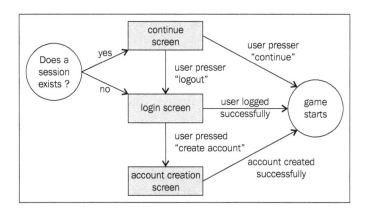

Each of those screens will be a `div` holding a few input fields and/or buttons. For example, the screen that lets the player create an account would be:

```
<div id="create" class="screen">
    <h1>Create an account</h1>
    <div class="input"><span>name:</span><input id="create-name"
type="text" /></div>
    <div class="input"><span>pw:</span><input id="create-pw"
type="text" /></div>
    <a class="button left" id="create-cancel" href="#">cancel</a>
    <a class="button right" id="create-create" href="#">create</a>
</div>
```

It will be styled with CSS and the interactive part will be written in jQuery. For this screen, the code is as follows:

```
$("#create-cancel").click(function(e){
    $("#create").css("display","none");
    $("#login").css("display","block");
    e.preventDefault();
});
$("#create-create").click(function(e){
    // interact with the server
    e.preventDefault();
});
```

The ID of the link used to connect the JavaScript code to the HTML code has been highlighted. Nothing too fancy, but it does the trick.

The interesting part has been intentionally left out of the preceding code, that is, the actual interaction with the server. All the interactions between our client (the game running into a browser) and the server will be done using JSON and the $.getJSON function that we talked about in the last chapter (this is a shorthand for $.ajax).

To transmit information to the server, we will use the second argument of the $.getJSON function. To transmit information to the client, the server will generate a JSON file.

We will use the server-side file to create an account called createUser.php, so the $.getJSON call will look as follows:

```
$.getJSON(
    "createUser.php",
    {
        name: $("#create-name").val(),
        pw: $("#create-pw").val()
    },
    handleCreateUserJson
)
```

As we've already mentioned, we submit the name and password the user chose by wrapping them in an object literal and pass it as the second argument to the function call. As already said, the third argument is a function that will handle the JSON file once the server returns it.

Searching elements in the database

For the first time, we will have to generate a JSON file. This one is pretty trivial; it should tell the client if the account creation was successful or not and if it is, the information about the player.

We've chosen to write it as the following code snippet, but it's really up to you to create the JSON files in a way that makes the most sense to you. If you are not familiar with the exact syntax a JSON file should follow, have a quick read at http://www.json.org/.

```
{
    "success" : true,
    "x" : 510,
    "y" : 360,
    "dir" : 0
}
```

It's quite easy to implement the function that will read this JSON file and react accordingly. We will launch the game if the operation is a success and display an error message if something went wrong. The following code does just that:

```
var handleCreateUserJson = function(json,status){
    if (json.success){
        name = $("#create-name").val();
        initialPlayerPos.x   = json.x;
        initialPlayerPos.y   = json.y;
        initialPlayerPos.dir = json.dir;
        $("#create").css("display","none");
        gf.startGame(initialize);
    } else {
        alert("Name already taken!");
    }
}
```

This is pretty simple as most of the complicated stuff is running on the server. Let's see what has to be done there. First, we have to retrieve the parameters sent by the client. As we use `$.getJSON`, the request to the JSON file is a GET request. This means that we will use PHP's `$_GET` super-global variable to access them. When passing sensible information to the server, you may want to use a POST request instead (though that alone won't prevent someone motivated enough to still access the parameters). `$_GET` is a variable that holds all the parameters sent by the client, so in our case, we can write:

```
$name = $_GET['name'];
$pw   = $_GET['pw'];
```

We will have stored the name and password the user chose into variables. Now we have to probe the database to check if a user with this name isn't already defined. To run a SQL query in PHP, we will use mysqli (`http://php.net/manual/en/book.mysqli.php`):

```
// 1) contect to the DB server
$link = mysqli_connect('localhost', 'username', 'password');

// Select the DB
mysqli_select_db($link, 'rpg');

// query the DB
$result = mysqli_query($link, 'SELECT * FROM players WHERE name =
"'.$name.'"');
```

> Note that the preceding code is not to be used for production as we directly insert the parameters provided by the user into the database query and that creates a huge risk of SQL injection! The best practice would be to always escape all the strings before injecting them into SQL queries. A simple way would be to use mysqli_escape (`http://www.php.net/manual/en/mysqli.real-escape-string.php`).

We won't go into the detail of writing the SQL query. They are pretty easy to read and, for a basic query like this one, to write. If you want to learn more about SQL, you can search the Web or read one of the many books available on the subject.

Once we have the result of the query, we need to check if the query returned an element to see if the name was already present in the DB. This is simply done with:

```
$obj = mysqli_fetch_object($result);
```

Now, if $obj is zero, we can create the new account.

Creating a new player in the database

Before looking at the query that will create the player in the database let's talk about passwords. You should never store raw passwords in the database because history has shown that databases get hacked quite often. The recommended solution is to hash the password before storing it. Then you can simply compare the hashed version of the submitted password with the one stored in the database.

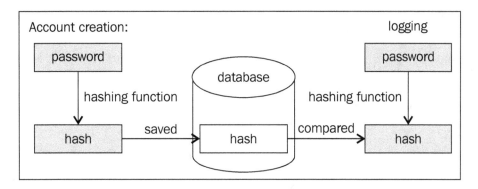

That's what we will do here with PHP's `hash` function. Then we will simply insert the username and the hash into the database along with the starting position of the player.

As this is also a query, we use the exact same function we used to find out if an account already existed with this name:

```
$hash = hash('md5', $pw);
$query = 'INSERT INTO players (name, x, y, dir, pw, state)
VALUES ("'.$name.'", 510, 360, 0, "'.$hash.'", 0)';
mysqli_query($link, $query);
```

The first argument that we passed to the `hash` function is highlighted in the preceding code. It's the hash method, and the `'md5'` that we used here is not recommended for production because it's considered too easy to break nowadays. If you want to find out more about what methods are available, have a look at the function documentation at `http://www.php.net/manual/en/function.hash.php`.

Now we can generate the JSON that the client will receive. This is done by using PHP's `json_encode` function (`http://php.net/manual/en/function.json-encode.php`). This function takes an object and transforms it into a JSON-formatted string.

```
$json['success'] = true;
$json['x'] = 510;
$json['y'] = 360;
$json['dir'] = 0;

echo json_encode($json);
```

Now, just to give you a global picture of what the client file looks like. The complete code is reproduced as follows:

```php
<?php
    session_start();

    include 'dbconnect.php';

    // JSON Object
    $json = array('success'=>false);

    $name = $_GET['name'];
    $pw   = $_GET['pw'];

    if(isset($name) && isset($pw)) {
        $hash = hash('md5', $pw);
        $query = 'SELECT * FROM players WHERE name = "'.$name.'"';
        $result = mysqli_query($link, $query);
        $obj = mysqli_fetch_object($result);
        if(!$obj){
            $query = 'INSERT INTO players (name, x, y, dir, pw, state)
VALUES("'.$name.'", 510, 360, 0, "'.$hash.'", 0)';
            $result = mysqli_query($link, $query);

            $_SESSION['name'] = $name;
            $_SESSION['pw'] = $pw;

                $json['success'] = true;
                $json['x'] = 510;
                $json['y'] = 360;
                $json['dir'] = 0;
        }
    }

    echo json_encode($json);

    // Close DB's connection
    mysqli_close($link);
?>
```

Here, you can see that we are including a file called dbconnect.php, which allows us to write the database configuration only once in this file and use it from every file that needs to connect to it. This is the same basic function we will use for every other functionality we will implement server side.

Keeping the player connected

There is, however, one thing in this implementation that we haven't explained yet. If you look at the highlighted code, you will see that the name of the user is stored into the session.

This will allow the server to continue knowing the name of the player without having to submit it with every following request. It will also allow us to permit the user to continue playing the game without having to give his/her username and password again if he/she comes back while the session is still valid.

If you look at the user-interaction flow graph at the beginning of this chapter, you will see there is a screen that proposes to the user to continue playing. We will display it only if the server still has a valid session it can use for him/her. To check this, we will create another PHP file named `session.php` that looks as follows:

```php
<?php
    session_start();

    // MySQL connection
    include 'dbconnect.php';

    // JSON Object
    $json = array('connected'=>'false');

    if(isset($_SESSION['name'])) {
        $query = 'SELECT * FROM players WHERE name = "'.$_
SESSION['name'].'"';
        $result = mysqli_query($link, $query);
        $obj = mysqli_fetch_object($result);
        if($obj){
            $json['name'] = $_SESSION['name'];
            $json['x'] = floatval($obj->x);
            $json['y'] = floatval($obj->y);
            $json['dir'] = intval($obj->dir);
        } else {
          session_destroy();
        }

        mysqli_free_result($result);
    }

    echo json_encode($json);

    mysqli_close($link);
?>
```

Then we simply check if the name is present in the session. However, if it is, there is one more thing we need to do; that is, retrieve the player from the database. This will give us its last coordinate and check once more that the username and password really match.

We don't save the coordinate in the session itself because we want the player to be able to connect to the same account using many different machines or browsers (although not simultaneously).

Once a request has been executed by the database, we can use mysql_result to read the result. This function takes three arguments:

1. The result of the query, generated by mysql_query.
2. The index of the result we want to read. This is needed because a query can return more than one result (for example, if we search for all the accounts in the players table).
3. The name of the field we want to read.

Once we have this information, we can send it to the client by formatting it into a JSON file.

On the client side, we will call this function at the very beginning of the game to choose which screen to display (the continue screen or the login one). This is done as usual with a $.getJSON call.

```
$.getJSON(
    "session.php",
    function(json){
        if(json.connected){
            name = json.name;
            initialPlayerPos.x   = json.x;
            initialPlayerPos.y   = json.y;
            initialPlayerPos.dir = json.dir;
            $("#session-name").html(name);
            $("#session").show(0);
        } else {
            $("#login").show(0);
        }
    }
);
```

This is very similar to what we have done before.

Logging the user into the game

This is done in almost the exact same way we checked for an existing session. On the server side, we need to make a request to prove if the username and password match and get the player position.

On the client side, we need to display a warning if the password was wrong and start the game if everything went well.

The JSON we use for this is as follows:

```
{
    "success" : true ,
    "x" : 154,
    "y" : 1043,
    "dir" :0
};
```

If the username and password don't match, success will be false. Otherwise, the JSON will look as shown earlier. We won't show you the server and client-side code as they are very similar to what we have already seen.

Keeping the players in sync

With what we've seen until now, we can log into the game, but that's about it; what we need now is a way to keep the server informed of the player's movement and to give the client the position of all the other players. The following figure shows you how the client and the server will interact:

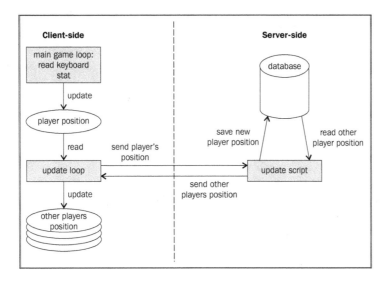

We will do both these things in one JSON call. We will use it to pass to the server the player's current position as we did before for the username and password. In return, the server will generate a JSON file with the list of all the other players.

```
{
    "players" : [
        {"name": "Alice", "x": 23, "y": 112, "dir": 0, "state": 0},
        {"name": "Bob", "x": 1004, "y": 50, "dir": 2, "state": 1}
    ]
};
```

Let's first have a look at the server side. There we need to write two queries: the first one to retrieve the list of all players and the second one to update the state of the current player.

Retrieving all the other players

This simply means finding all the entries in the `players` table except the one for the current player. There is, however, one thing we have to be careful about: we only want to display the players that are currently playing the game.

As a lot of things can happen online, we cannot be sure that the player will be able to log out before being disconnected, so instead, we choose to use a time stamp. Each time that the player updates its position, we will set the time stamp to the current time.

This way we can know which players are not online anymore by comparing this time stamp to the current time. We've arbitrarily decided that player will be considered offline if we haven't heard from him/her in more than 10 minutes. The corresponding MySQL query would be:

```
$query = 'SELECT * FROM players WHERE lastupdate >
TIMESTAMPADD(MINUTE, -10, NOW()) AND name <> "'.$_GET['name'].'"';
```

Here, we test if the name is not the same as the current player (`<>` means "not equal to" in SQL).

The code that reads the result and prints it to the server's response is as follows:

```
$result = mysqli_query($link, $query);

while ($obj = mysqli_fetch_object($result)) {
    array_push($json['players'], array('name'=>$obj->name,
'x'=>floatval($obj->x), 'y'=>floatval($obj->y), 'dir'=>intval($obj-
>dir), 'state'=>floatval($obj->state)));
```

```
    }

    mysqli_free_result($result);
```

This is very similar to when we retrieve just the current user from the database, so you should already be familiar with this code.

Updating the current player position

To update the entry in the database that holds the information about the player, we can use the following query:

```
mysqli_query($link, 'UPDATE players SET x='.$x.', y ='.$y.',
dir = '.$dir.', state = '.$state.', lastupdate = NOW() WHERE
name="'.$name.'"');
```

As we don't expect any result from this query, we don't need to store it anywhere.

Client-side code

Now we need to write the code that will send the current player position to the server. This is not too complicated as it's just passing the parameters to the $.getJSON call. We will, however, need to encode the player direction and status to integers (as we decided to store them that way in the database).

To do this, we will extend the player's object with two new methods:

```
this.getState = function(){
    switch (state){
        case "idle":
            return 0;
        case "walk":
            return 1;
        case "strike":
            return 2;
        default:
            return 0;
    }
};

this.getOrientation = function(){
    switch (orientation){
        case "down":
            return 0;
        case "up":
```

```
                 return 1;
           case "left":
                 return 2;
           default:
                 return 3;
     }
};
```

Then, we will simply call them when we call getJSON:

```
$.getJSON(
    "update.php",
    {
        name: name,
        x: gf.x(player.div),
        y: gf.y(player.div),
        dir: player.getOrientation(),
        state: player.getState()
    },
    updateOthers
);
```

The callback function is probably the most complicated part of this whole chapter. Go through the returned list of all players. If a new player was created, we need to add him/her to the map. If a player moved, we need to update his/her position, and if a player quit the game, we need to remove him/her.

This is exactly what the following code does:

```
function(json,status){
    // Here we need to update the position of all the other players
    var existingOthers = {};
    var players = json.players
    for (var i = 0; i < players.length; i++){
        var other = players[i];
        existingOthers["other_"+other.name] = true;
        var avatar, weapon;
        var div = $("#other_"+other.name);
        var created = false;
        if(div.size() > 0){
            avatar = $("#other_"+other.name+"_avatar");
            weapon = $("#other_"+other.name+"_weapon");
            // update
            gf.x(div, other.x);
            gf.y(div, other.y);
            div.css("z-index",other.y + 160);
```

```
        } else {
          var created = true;
          // create other players
          div = gf.addGroup($("#others"), "other_"+other.name, {
              x:        other.x,
              y:        other.y
          })
          others.push( div );
          div.css("z-index",other.y + 160);
          avatar = gf.addSprite(div, "other_"+other.name+"_avatar", {
              x:        (192-128)/2,
                y:        (192-128)/2,
                width:  128,
                height: 128
          });
          weapon = gf.addSprite(div, "other_"+other.name+"_weapon", {
                width:  192,
                height: 192
            });
          div.append("<div style='font-family: \"Press Start 2P\";
background: rgba(0,0,0,0.5); padding: 5px; color: #FFF; width: 192px;
position: absolute;'>"+other.name+"</div>");
          div.data("state", {dir: other.dir, state: other.state});
        }

      // set the correct animation
      if(created || other.state !== div.data("state").state || other.
dir !== div.data("state").dir){
          div.data("state", {dir: other.dir, state: other.state});

          gf.transform(avatar, {flipH: false});
          gf.transform(weapon, {flipH: false});
          var pAnim =  playerAnim.stand;
          var wAnim =  weaponAnim.stand;
          if(other.state === 1){
              pAnim = playerAnim.walk;
            wAnim = weaponAnim.walk;
          } else if (other.state === 2){
              pAnim = playerAnim.strike;
            wAnim = weaponAnim.strike;
          }
          if(other.dir === 0){
              gf.setAnimation(avatar, pAnim.down, true);
              gf.setAnimation(weapon, wAnim.down, true);
```

```
            } else if (other.dir === 1){
               gf.setAnimation(avatar, pAnim.up, true);
               gf.setAnimation(weapon, wAnim.up, true);
            } else {
               gf.setAnimation(avatar, pAnim.side, true);
               gf.setAnimation(weapon, wAnim.side, true);
               if(other.dir === 2){
                  gf.transform(avatar, {flipH: true});
                  gf.transform(weapon, {flipH: true});
               }
            }
         }


      }
      // remove gone others
      for (var i = others.length-1; i >= 0; i--){
         var other = others[i];
         if(!existingOthers[other.attr("id")]){
            other.fadeOut(2000, function(){
                  $(this).remove();
            });
            others.splice(i,1);
         }
      }
   }

   setTimeout(updateFunction,100);
}
```

The first part is to either update the position or create the other players. The second part is to set the correct animation based on the player orientation and status.

Then we go through the list of all players and if some of them weren't on the list of updated players, we remove them from the game.

Finally, we set a timeout for the function calling $.getJSON to be called again in 100 milliseconds. The frequency you choose will be a trade-off between server usage and game fluidity, so you probably will have to fine-tune this value to your game needs.

Taking care of monsters

Now the game starts to get interesting. There is, however, one small thing missing. If one player kills a monster, it will only be dead for him and not for all the other players. This can be fine in some very special cases, but most of the time this is not what we want.

The solution is to implement the logic that takes care of the enemies and the fights server side. This means that we need another database table that will hold all of our enemies. This table will need to hold the following information:

- The ID of the enemy, to identify it uniquely
- The type of the enemy — a skeleton, an ogre, and so on — to define how it will look to the player
- The x and y coordinate of the enemy
- Its life to allow the player to kill it
- Its defense for the combat system
- Its spawn rate to determine when the monster should be spawned again once it has been killed

Then, periodically, we will transmit to the clients the position and properties of those enemies. As we already have a page that is being pooled regularly to get the position of the other players, we can simply enhance it to return the state of the enemies too.

This simply means that the JSON file will now look like this (with the new part highlighted):

```json
{
    "players" : [
        {"name": "Alice", "x": 23, "y": 112, "dir": 0, "state": 0},
        {"name": "Bob", "x": 1004, "y": 50, "dir": 2, "state": 1}
    ],
    "enemies" : [
        {"name": "enemy1", "type" : "ogre", "x": 2014, "y": 200},
        {"name": "enemy2", "type" : "skeleton", "x": 220, "y": 560}
    ]
};
```

We will need another query to find all the enemies still alive in the database:

```sql
SELECT * FROM enemies WHERE life <> 0
```

The code that writes the JSON and parses it to create or update the enemies is exactly the same as the one for the other players, so we won't reproduce it here, but you can have a look at the full source if you want to.

Implementing server-side combat

To implement combat with those server-side enemies, we could still use the code we have client side and send the result to the server. This has some serious disadvantages, as it is very easy to cheat the system and modify the client to simply send the information that the enemy has been defeated without really doing the combat. Secondly, it makes dealing with combat between one enemy and many players very difficult.

We will instead implement it server side, as it is shown in the following diagram:

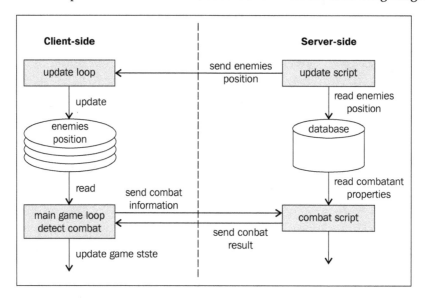

The code that used to get executed client side was as follows:

```
this.detectInteraction = function(npcs, enemies, console){
    if(state == "strike" && !interacted){
        // ... interaction with NPCs here ...
        for (var i = 0; i < enemies.length; i++){
            if(gf.spriteCollide(this.hitzone, enemies[i].div)){
                var enemyRoll = enemies[i].object.defend();
                var playerRoll = Math.round(Math.random() * 6) + 5;

                if(enemyRoll <= playerRoll){
                    var dead = enemies[i].object.kill(playerRoll);
                    console.html("You hit the enemy
"+playerRoll+"pt");
```

```
            if (dead) {
                console.html("You killed the enemy!");
                enemies[i].div.fadeOut(2000, function(){
                    $(this).remove();
                });
                enemies.splice(i,1);
            }
        } else {
            console.html("The enemy countered your attack");
        }
        interacted = true;
        return;
    }
  }
}
```

We will now simply have a JSON call:

```
this.detectInteraction = function(npcs, enemies, console){
    if(state == "strike" && !interacted){
        // ... interaction with NPCs here ...
        for (var i = 0; i < enemies.length; i++){
            if(gf.spriteCollide(this.hitzone, enemies[i])){
                $.getJSON("fight.php",
                    { name : enemies[i].attr("id") },
                    function(json){
                        if (json.hit){
                            if (json.success){
                                if(json.killed){
                                    console.html("You killed the enemy!");
                                } else {
                                    console.html("You hit the enemy
"+json.damage+"pt");
                                }
                            } else {
                                console.html("The enemy countered your
attack");
                            }
                        }
                    })
                interacted = true;
                return;
            }
        }
    }
};
```

Here, you can see that the JSON contains two flags to give information about the combat. The first is `hit`; it is true if the combat really happened. This is necessary because there is a chance that the enemy is already dead without the client knowing it. Then, `success` conveys the success of the attack and is `false` if the enemy successfully defended itself and `true` otherwise.

The complete logic of the combat will be implemented server side in the `fight.php` file, but is the exact replica of what used to happen client side:

```php
$query = 'SELECT * FROM enemies WHERE life <> 0 AND name =
"'.$name.'"';
$result = mysqli_query($link, $query);
$obj = mysqli_fetch_object($result);
if ($obj) {

    $playerRoll = rand ( 5 , 11 );
    $enemyRoll  = rand ( $obj->defense, $obj->defense + 6);

    $json['hit'] = true;

    if ($playerRoll > $enemyRoll){
        $json['success'] = true;

        if($playerRoll > $obj->life){
            $json['killed'] = true;

            // update DB
            mysqli_query($link, 'UPDATE enemies SET life = 0 WHERE
name = "'.$name.'"');
        } else {
            $json['killed'] = false;
            $json['damage'] = intval($playerRoll);

            // update DB
            mysqli_query($link, 'UPDATE enemies SET life = '.($obj-
>life - $playerRoll).' WHERE name = "'.$name.'"');
        }
    }
}
```

The highlighted part represents the code that was taken out of the client and put into the server. And that's all you really need for the combat to work.

Once an enemy is dead, you may want to periodically respawn it. The most obvious way is to use a server-side script that gets executed at regular intervals through the use of a `cron` command. Alternatively, you could cheat and use any of the other files we created to respawn the enemies; for example, each time a player logs in.

Summary

The game we've created here is by far the most complex we've written in this book so far. It could of course be enhanced a lot by adding PvP combat, a chat system, and so on, but this chapter has covered all the basics to allow you to implement those!

However, calling a bunch of files asynchronously is not a very elegant solution, and if you target very recent browsers, you may want to take a look at the WebSocket API that allows you to establish and maintain a bi-directional communication channel between the browser and the server.

Another way to maintain a permanent connection to the server is by using long polling methods.

In the next chapter, we will modify our platformer to integrate with Facebook and Twitter as well as keep a list of high scores!

8
Let's Get Social

Since the time of the first videogame, a simple technique has been used to keep them interesting — **leaderboards**. Leaderboards are a simple way to keep the players playing your game. The players will try to perform better each time, better than their friends, or better than any other players in the world.

Social networks add a new dimension to this simple idea by allowing the game to publish the player score to his/her timeline (or feed). This has many advantages, one of them being that it will help potential new players to learn about your game. If they see that one of their friends just played your game, then they may want to try it too!

In this chapter, we will first show how to implement a simple server-side leaderboard using the same techniques we saw in the previous chapter. We will then see how to allow the player to log in with his/her Twitter account into the game and tweet the score on his/her behalf.

Finally, we will see how to log in to the game using Facebook, publish events in the player's timeline, and create achievements.

It's important to realize when you use Facebook or Twitter that you have to be careful to follow the rules they establish, and even stay informed about the change of the rules to keep your game compliant. It's been seen more than once that applications or games that were previously allowed to use those services were then banned.

We will show you how to use these two social networks, but the base mechanisms are the same for almost any service around that provides the same kind of functionality.

We will cover these subjects in the following order:

- Creating a simple self-hosted leaderboard
- Making cheating harder
- Integrating the game with Twitter to allow the player to tweet his/her score
- Integrating the game with Facebook to allow the player to win achievements

Creating a simple leaderboard

Obviously, creating a leaderboard will require some sort of database to keep a tab of the scores. As in the previous chapter, we will use PHP and MySQL to implement the server side of our game. However, unlike in *Chapter 7, Making a Multiplayer Game*, playing together the solution presented here can be viable in real life. Requesting and saving highscores is an operation that takes very little server resources and isn't called that often; for each user, we will approximately query the server once every 10 seconds, as opposed to where we queried it many times per second for our MMORPG in *Chapter 7, Making a Multiplayer Game*.

First, we will need a metric to use as a score. Here, we will simply use the time it took for the player to finish a level, in seconds. The following diagram shows the user interaction workflow that we will use:

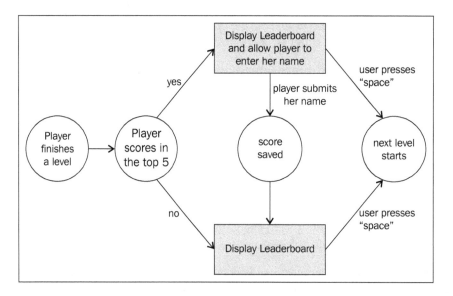

As a UI, we will use two screens that we will implement in the same way we implemented the interface for the last chapter—simple `div` elements that we will make visible or invisible, as we need them.

The first screen is simply there to announce the beginning of a level and prompt the user to get ready. The second one is more complex. It shows the result of the player, the list of the top five players, and if the player scored amongst them, give him/her the opportunity to save his/her name into this list. The following screenshot shows what this will look like:

We chose to use this mechanism instead of asking for the user's name at the beginning of the game, and then automatically save the score because this mimics the behavior of old arcade games.

This means there are two server-side actions:

1. Retrieving the top five list of scores for a level.
2. Saving a score for a given level.

We will implement those two actions with two files, namely, highscore.php and save.php.

Saving highscores

The database table we will use holds three columns:

- Level: This is an integer that holds the index of the level
- Name: This is a string that holds the username
- Time: This is an integer that represents the number of seconds it took the user to finish the level

The script that saves the highscore is very simple—we will transmit the name, score, and level to the server. We will then save them to the database with the following SQL query:

```
INSERT INTO scores (level, name, time) VALUES (1, "John", 36)
```

The rest of the script is very similar to what we saw in the previous chapter, so we won't reproduce it here, but you can have a look at the full source code if you want.

Retrieving highscores

To retrieve the highscores, you can simply provide the level to the server and get the scores in return, but we have chosen a slightly more complex mechanism. We will give the task of deciding if the current user is part of the top five list, and if so, at which position. This will allow you to implement anti-cheating measures later.

So, you will provide the level and user's time to the server and it will return a JSON file holding all the information you need to generate the leaderboard screen. We chose the following format for the JSON:

```
{
  "top" : [
    {"name": "Joe", "time": 14},
    {"name": "John", "time": 15},
    {"time": 17},
    {"name": "Anna", "time": 19}
  ],
  "intop": true,
  "pos": 2
}
```

The idea here is to have a flag to indicate that the player is in the top five list, `intop`. If this flag is true, then another variable named `pos` is present too. This variable holds the index in the array, `top`, that holds the player's time. All the other entries in `top` are the scores of players in the leaderboard, sorted from the first to the fifth. If `intop` is false, the array only holds the other player's scores.

To generate this response, we will first use a SQL query:

```
SELECT * FROM scores WHERE level=1 ORDER BY time ASC LIMIT 5
```

This query starts like the other queries we used up until now, but at the end (highlighted in the preceding code above), it is a modifier that specifies that you want the result sorted by ascending times (`ORDER BY time ASC`) and that we only want five results (`LIMIT 5`).

There is not much work to do to parse the result and generate the JSON. The only subtlety is the insertion of the player's score if it is good enough. Here is the complete code for this page:

```php
<?php
  session_start();

  include 'dbconnect.php';

  $time = $_GET['time'];
  $level = $_GET['level'];

  if(isset($time) && isset($level)){

    // JSON Object
    $json = array('top'=>array(), 'intop'=>false);

    $query = 'SELECT * FROM scores WHERE level='.$level.' ORDER BY
time ASC LIMIT 5';
    $result = mysqli_query($link, $query);
    $i=0;

    while ($obj = mysqli_fetch_object($result)) {
      if(!$json['intop'] && $time < $obj->time){
        $json['intop'] = true;
        $json['pos'] = $i;

        array_push($json['top'], array('time'=>$time));

        $i++;
      }
      if($i < 5){
        array_push($json['top'], array('time'=>$obj->time,
'name'=>$obj->name));
        $i++;
      }
    }

    if($i < 5 && !$json['intop']){
      $json['intop'] = true;
      $json['pos'] = $i;

      array_push($json['top'], array('time'=>$time));
    }

    mysqli_free_result($result);
```

```
      echo json_encode($json);
   }

   mysqli_close($link);
?>
```

The highlighted parts of this code are the ones that take care of the player's score.

Displaying the highscores

On the client side, we will generate the screen with the result and an input field to allow the player to submit its name to the leaderboard, if he/she so wishes. Let's have a look at the code that does this:

```
var finishedTime = Math.round((Date.now() - levelStart) / 1000);
   $.ajax({
      dataType: "json",
      url: "highscore.php",
      data: {
         level: currentLevel,
         time: finishedTime
      },
      async: false,
      success: function (json) {
         var top = "";
         for (var i = 0; i < json.top.length; i++){
            if(json.intop && json.pos === i){
               top += "<input id='name' placeholder='_____' size='5' />"
                  + "<input id='timeScore' type='hidden' value='"+json.
top[i].time+"'></input>"
                  + "<input id='level' type='hidden'
value='"+currentLevel+"'></input>"
                  + " "+minSec(json.top[i].time)
                  + " <a id='saveScore' href='#'>submit</a> <br>";
            } else {
               top += "" + json.top[i].name + " " + minSec(json.top[i].
time) + "<br>";
            }
         }
         $("#top_list").html(top);
      }
   }).fail(function(a,b,c){
      var toto = "toto";
   });
```

The code that generates the list itself is highlighted. Here, we create three input fields — one for the player to enter his/her name and two hidden ones to hold the level number and the player score. They are followed by a link that will be used to submit the score. The code that handles the link is as follows:

```
$("#levelEnd").on("click","#saveScore",function(){
    $.get("save.php",{
        name: $("#name").val(),
        time: $("#timeScore").val(),
        level: $("#level").val()
    }, function(){
        $("#saveScore").fadeOut(500);
    });
    return false;
});
```

Here, we simply retrieve the values of the input fields and then submit them to the server. As a small feedback to the player, we remove the submit button once it's done.

Making cheating harder

There is no silver bullet to avoid a cheater in general. This is particularly true with games written in JavaScript, since their source code is so easy to access. Of course, you can obfuscate your code, but that will only slow down someone really motivated to figure out your code. There are, however, a few other techniques that you can use to make it more difficult or less efficient to cheat in your game.

Server-side verification

The safest way to prevent cheating is to move things on the server side. If you remember, that's exactly what we did with the fight mechanism in our MMORPG in *Chapter 7, Making a Multiplayer Game*. To apply the same paradigm to a platformer would effectively mean transmitting every keystroke to the server and letting the server decide the resulting position for the player.

In most cases, this is not a realistic solution. But you can still use the server-side logic to validate the score submitted by the player. You can have a series of invisible checkpoints distributed in the level where you ping the server. If the user submits a score without having passed through each of those, then something fishy is going on. You can also record a series of metrics, such as how many times the player dies or jumps.

The thing is that you must really tailor the validation for your game; there is no general approach. However, it is very important that your anti-cheating measures don't flag an honest player as a cheater, because that will generate a lot of frustration. It's also important for you to think about how much effort you want to invest in this area, since the more time you spend on this, the less the time you will spend on your game's other areas.

For your game, we will implement something simple. We know how fast the player is moving, we know how far the end of the level is, so we can compute a minimum time it will take the player to go through the level. We will compare the player's score to this and validate it if it's not smaller.

To do this, we will simply add those lines in `highscore.php`:

```
// player walk may 7px in 30ms -> 233.1
$minTime = array(
  1 => 15, // 3500 / 233.1
  2 => 15, // 3500 / 233.1
  3 => 42, // 9800 / 233.1
  4 => 23 // 5460 / 233.1
);
$timeValid = !($minTime[intval($level)] < intval($time));
//...
while ($obj = mysqli_fetch_object($result)) {
  if(!$json['intop'] && $time < $obj->time && $timeValid){
    // ...
  }
}
```

If the player score was detected as `impossible`, it will still be displayed, but the player won't be prompted to enter his/her name.

Making your variables less readable

One thing you can do is make it harder for someone to cheat your game simply by opening the browser's inspector and changing a value somewhere, since we used the hidden input field to store values before sending them back to the server, to save the highscore. This makes sense in a strictly semantic way and makes our server-side implementation rest, but is very easy to hack. The following screenshot shows what a user would see if he/she opens the page in Chrome's page inspector:

One simple rule of thumb is to avoid storing any important information in the DOM, since it's accessible to any user, even those without much programming knowledge. In our case, we will simply remove those from the call to save.php and use the session to store the values instead. In highscore.php, we can simply add the following code:

```
if(!$json['intop'] && $time < $obj->time && $timeValid){
  $json['intop'] = true;
  $json['pos'] = $i;

  array_push($json['top'], array('time'=>$time));

  $_SESSION['level'] = $level;
  $_SESSION['time'] = $time;

  $i++;
}
```

The save.php file only has to look for the level and time into the session:

```
$name = $_GET['name'];
$time = $_SESSION['time'];
$level = $_SESSION['level'];
```

This simple change already makes the game harder to cheat.

Obfuscating your code

Obfuscating your code is a very simple step, but will help you quite a lot. Once your code is obfuscated, it will be almost unreadable in the inspector. The following example is a piece of code that asks for the leaderboard:

```
if (status == "finished") {
  gameState = "menu";
  $("#level_nb_2").html(currentLevel);
  $("#level_nb_1").html(currentLevel + 1);

  var finishedTime = Math.round((Date.now() - levelStart) / 1000);
  $.ajax({
    dataType: "json",
    url: "highscore.php",
    data: {
      level: currentLevel,
      time: finishedTime
    },
    async: false,
    success: function (json) {
      var top = "";
      for (var i = 0; i < json.top.length; i++){
        if(json.intop && json.pos === i){
          top += "<input id='name' placeholder='_____' size='5' />"
            + "<input id='timeScore' type='hidden' value='"+json.
top[i].time+"'></input>"
            + "<input id='level' type='hidden'
value='"+currentLevel+"'></input>"
            + " "+minSec(json.top[i].time)
            + " <a id='saveScore' href='#'>submit</a> <br>";
        } else {
          top += "" + json.top[i].name + " " + minSec(json.top[i].
time) + "<br>";
        }
      }
      $("#top_list").html(top);
    }
```

```
  }).fail(function(a,b,c){
    var toto = "toto";
  });

  $("#time").html(minSec(finishedTime));

  $("#levelEnd").fadeIn(2000, function(){
    $("#backgroundFront").css("background-position","0px 0px");
    $("#backgroundBack").css("background-position","0px 0px");
    gf.x(group, 0);

    tilemap = loadNextLevel(group);
    gf.x(player.div, 0);
    gf.y(player.div, 0);
    gf.setAnimation(player.div, playerAnim.jump);
  });
  status = "stand";
}
```

The same code once obfuscated (through UglifyJS) looks similar to the following:

```
if("finished"==status){gameState="menu",$("#level_nb_2").
html(currentLevel),$("#level_nb_1").html(currentLevel+1);var
finishedTime=Math.round((Date.now()-levelStart)/1e3);$.ajax({dataType
:"json",url:"highscore.php",data:{level:currentLevel,time:finishedTim
e},async:!1,success:function(a){for(var b="",c=0;a.top.length>c;c++)
b+=a.intop&&a.pos===c?"<input id='name' placeholder='_____' size='5'
/><input id='timeScore' type='hidden' value='"+a.top[c].time+"'></
input>"+"<input id='level' type='hidden' value='"+currentLevel+"'></
input>"+" "+minSec(a.top[c].time)+" <a id='saveScore'
href='#'>submit</a> <br>":""+a.top[c].name+" "+minSec(a.top[c].
time)+"<br>";$("#top_list").html(b)}}).fail(function(){}),$("#time").
html(minSec(finishedTime)),$("#levelEnd").fadeIn(2e3,function()
{$("#backgroundFront").css("background-position","0px
0px"),$("#backgroundBack").css("background-position","0px 0px"),gf.x(
group,0),tilemap=loadNextLevel(group),gf.x(player.div,0),gf.y(player.
div,0),gf.setAnimation(player.div,playerAnim.jump)}),status="stand"}
```

This is already way more difficult to debug and at the same time, it's smaller!

Making your network protocol less readable

Once the client side of the code is fixed, there is still a place where a cheater could access the game variable — network traffic. Let's have a look at what a sniffing application can see when the player finishes the level:

```
       6 0.000548000   localhost              localhost              TCP       76 ddi-tcp-1 > 50241 [A
       7 0.006098000   localhost              localhost              HTTP      472 HTTP/1.1 200 OK  (te
       8 0.006140000   localhost              localhost              TCP       76 50241 > ddi-tcp-1 [A
▷ Frame 5: 631 bytes on wire (5048 bits), 631 bytes captured (5048 bits) on interface 0
▷ Null/Loopback
▷ Internet Protocol Version 6, Src: localhost (::1), Dst: localhost (::1)
▷ Transmission Control Protocol, Src Port: 50241 (50241), Dst Port: ddi-tcp-1 (8888), Seq: 1, Ack: 1, Len: 555
▽ Hypertext Transfer Protocol
   ▷ GET /book/code/chapter%208/save.php?name=Test&time=18&level=1 HTTP/1.1\r\n
     Host: localhost:8888\r\n
     Connection: keep-alive\r\n
     Accept: */*\r\n

     User-Agent: Mozilla/5.0 (Macintosh; Intel Mac OS X 10_8_2) AppleWebKit/537.17 (KHTML, like Gecko) Chrome/24.0.

00c0  0d 0a 41 63 63 65 70 74  3a 20 2a 2f 2a 0d 0a        ..Accept : */*..
00d0
00e0
00f0     55 73 65 72 2d 41 67   65 6e 74 3a 20 4d 6f 7a    User-Ag ent: Moz
0100  69 6c 6c 61 2f 35 2e 30  20 28 4d 61 63 69 6e 74    illa/5.0  (Macint
0110  6f 73 68 3b 20 49 6e 74  65 6c 20 4d 61 63 20 4f    osh; Int el Mac O
0120  53 20 58 20 31 30 5f 38  5f 32 29 20 41 70 70 6c    S X 10_8 _2) Appl
0130  65 57 65 62 4b 69 74 2f  35 33 37 2e 31 37 20 28    eWebKit/ 537.17 (
0140  4b 48 54 4d 4c 2c 20 6c  69 6b 65 20 47 65 63 6b    KHTML, l ike Geck
0150  6f 29 20 43 68 72 6f 6d  65 2f 32 34 2e 30 2e 31    o) Chrom e/24.0.1
0160  33 31 33 2e 35 33 20 53  61 66 61 72 69 2f 35 33    313.53 S afari/53
```

This is a problem since without even having to hack the client-side code, a player could simply forge a packet with the right information to cheat. Here are three simple things that you could do to make it more difficult for a cheater to understand your network traffic:

1. Give random names to the variables so that by simply looking at them, the cheater cannot find out what value they hold.

2. Encode the content of the variables. This is very useful for this situation, because here the user typically knows the value of his/her score. He/she will only have to look for the variable that holds it to find out what he/she has to modify.

3. Add a lot of random variables to make it harder to know which ones are really being used.

Like before, this will only make it slightly harder to cheat for a determined player but combined with all the other techniques in the following sections, it will probably discourage most of them. Let's implement each one of these.

Encoding values

Let's first begin by encoding the values. This can be done in lots of ways, some more secure than others. Here, our goal is really only to prevent the cheater from searching for his/her score in the list of values to identify which one holds it. So, we don't need any complex encoding. We will simply use a left shift (<< on the client) and then a right shift (>> on the server).

Here is the client-side code:

```
$.ajax({
  dataType: "json",
  url: "highscore.php",
  data: {
    level: currentLevel,
    time: finishedTime << 1
  },
  async: false,
  success: function (json) {
    // ...
  }
});
```

The server counterpart is as follows:

```
$time = intval($_GET['time']) >> 1;
```

To confuse the user even more, we will transmit the value in a clear manner in many other variables that won't be readable on the server side.

Randomly naming the variables

There is not much to explain here; just replace the name of the variable! If you're really paranoid, then you can change the variables each time you call the server, but that's not what we will do here. Here is the client-side code:

```
$.ajax({
  dataType: "json",
  url: "highscore.php",
  data: {
    Nmyzsf: currentLevel,
    WfBCLQ: finishedTime << 1
  },
```

```
    async: false,
    success: function (json) {
      // ...
    }
  });
```

The server-side code is as follows:

```
$time = intval($_GET['WfBCLQ']) >> 1;
$level = $_GET['Nmyzsf'];
```

Adding random variables

Now that the names of the variables don't convey their content anymore, it's very important that you create more variables, otherwise it's very easy to just try each of them to find out which one contains the score. Here is an example of what you could do on the client side:

```
$.ajax({
  dataType: "json",
  url: "highscore.php",
  data: {
    sXZZUj: Math.round(200*Math.random()),
    enHf8F: Math.round(200*Math.random()),
    eZnqBG: currentLevel,
    avFanB: Math.round(200*Math.random()),
    zkpCfb: currentLevel,
    PCXFTR: Math.round(200*Math.random()),
    Nmyzsf: currentLevel,
    FYGswh: Math.round(200*Math.random()),
    C3kaTz: finishedTime << 1,
    gU7buf: finishedTime,
    ykN65g: Math.round(200*Math.random()),
    Q5jUZm: Math.round(200*Math.random()),
    bb5d7V: Math.round(200*Math.random()),
    WTsrdm: finishedTime << 1,
    bCW5Dg: currentLevel,
    AFM8MN: Math.round(200*Math.random()),
    FUHt6K: Math.round(200*Math.random()),
    WfBCLQ: finishedTime << 1,
    d8mzVn: Math.round(200*Math.random()),
    bHxNpb: Math.round(200*Math.random()),
    MWcmCz: finishedTime,
    ZAat42: Math.round(200*Math.random())
  },
```

```
    async: false,
    success: function (json) {
      // ...
    }
  });
```

The server doesn't have to change anything, since those new variables are just ignored. There will be some things that you may want to do, such as duplicate values and use the player score on the variable that won't be used.

While doing these things, you have to be very careful to annotate the code so that you remember which variables are the correct ones!

Integrating with Twitter

Twitter is an amazing way to share simple information with other people. You may want to use it in two ways:

- Allow the player to log in, thus providing a unique username
- Allow the player to tweet his/her high score or progression in the game

You will now see two possibilities to integrate your game with it.

Twitter for dummies

There is a very simple way to use Twitter that doesn't even require you to use any kind of API. If the user is already logged in to Twitter, you can prompt him/her to submit a prewritten tweet, simply by opening a URL. This URL is formatted as follows:

```
http://twitter.com/home?status=Pre written status here!
```

The highlighted part of this address is the status you wrote for the player. What we could do in our game is to provide a `tweet this` link next to the **Submit** button on the leaderboard screen:

```
$.ajax({
  dataType: "json",
  url: "highscore.php",
  data: {
    // ...
  },
  async: false,
  success: function (json) {
    var top = "";
```

```
      for (var i = 0; i < json.top.length; i++) {
         if(json.intop && json.pos === i) {
            top += "<input id='name' placeholder='_____' size='5' />"
            + " "+minSec(json.top[i].time)
            + " <a id='saveScore' href='#'>submit</a>"
            + " <a id='tweetScore' target='_blank' href='http://twitter.
com/home?status="+escape("I've just finished level "+currentLevel+" in
YAP in "+minSec(json.top[i].time)+"!")+"'>tweet</a> <br>";
         } else {
            top += "" + json.top[i].name + " " + minSec(json.top[i].time)
+ "<br>";
         }
      }
      $("#top_list").html(top);
   }
});
```

The highlighted part is where the magic happens. You will notice that we used JavaScript's escape function to make sure the string we provided is formatted for a URL.

This method is very easy to implement, but has some limitations:

- If the user is not already logged in, he/she will have to do so before posting his/her tweet.

- You cannot access the user's Twitter handle to use it for the local leaderboard. This means that if the player wants to tweet and save his/her time, then the name will have to be entered here too.

- For each tweet, a new window is opened and the player will have to confirm it.

If you want to allow the user to log in and automatically publish tweets without having to open a new window each time, then you will have to use Twitter's API.

Full access to Twitter's API

The more complete solution to integrate with Twitter is to ask the user for permission to connect his/her account to the game. The basic mechanism for this uses **OAuth**, which is an open authentication standard supported by a lot of companies such as Twitter, Google, and Facebook.

To give the player the choice to log in using Twitter or not, we will slightly change the startup screen:

If the player clicks on **Start game**, then he/she will start to play. If he/she clicks on **Log in with Twitter**, then he/she will be prompted to authorize the game with Twitter and then return to the game's startup screen.

Registering your game with Twitter

Before doing anything else, you have to register your game with Twitter. To do this, you first need to log in to the Twitter developer's site (`https://dev.twitter.com`). Then, you can click on **My Application**:

Here, you can click on **Create a new application**, fill in all the required fields, and agree to the terms and conditions of **Rules of the Road**. Once this is done, you will be prompted with a screen that presents to you all the properties of your newly created application:

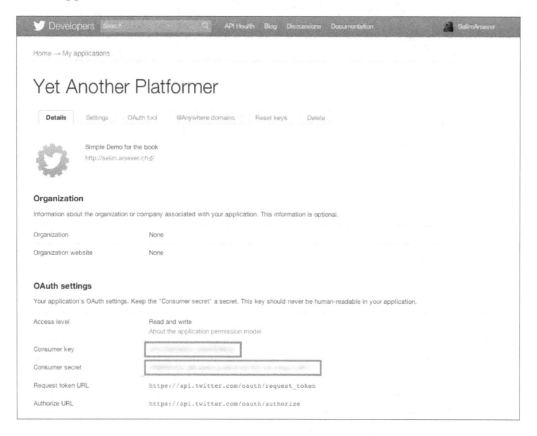

Please note the two areas of circled code in this screenshot; you'll need them later. There is one last thing that you will need to configure here. Go to the **Settings** tab and scroll down to **Application Type**. Here, by default, **Read only** is selected. If you want to be able to publish tweets on the user's behalf, you'll need to change this to **Read and Write**:

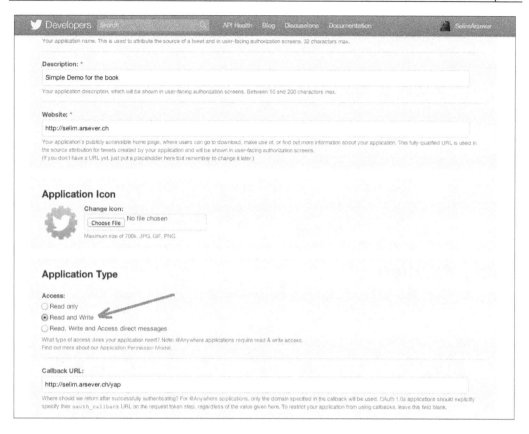

That's it; your game should now be configured correctly on Twitter's side.

Server-side helper library

You could implement all of the interactions with Twitter's API directly in PHP, but this would be tedious; thankfully, there exists a lot of libraries to help you with this. The one for PHP is called **twitteroauth** (`http://github.com/abraham/twitteroauth`). Other languages have other libraries, so don't hesitate to look at Twitter's developers' documentation to learn more about those.

The very nice thing about twitteroauth is that you can install it on almost every kind of hosting that supports PHP. You just need to copy the library's file in the same directory where you have your game's file. In our example, we copied them in a subdirectory called `twitter`.

Now, you need to configure the library. To do this, open `config.php` from the `twitteroauth` folder:

```
define('CONSUMER_KEY', '(1)');
define('CONSUMER_SECRET', '(2)');
define('OAUTH_CALLBACK', '(3)');
```

In this file, at (1) and (2), you have to write the two values that you noted previously in your application page on Twitter's developer website. Then, at (3), you have to write the URL of twitteroauth's `callback.php` file.

The very last step is to edit `callback.php` and to replace the following line with the address of your game's index file:

```
header('Location: ./index.php');
```

Authentication

Here is the workflow used to authenticate and authorize your game with Twitter:

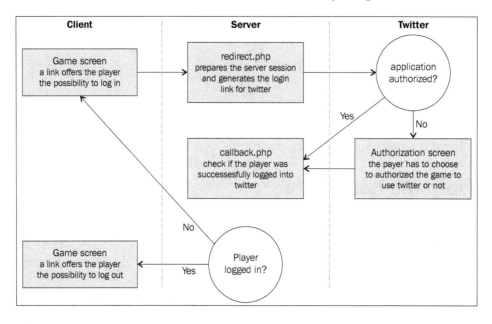

This is not as complicated as it looks, and a big part of this workflow is already implemented by twitteroauth. We will now create a login page with a **Twitter** button. We will use a simple link that points to twitteroauth's `redirect.php` file. When the player clicks on it for the first time, he/she will be redirected to a page on Twitter's website that asks him/her to authorize the game:

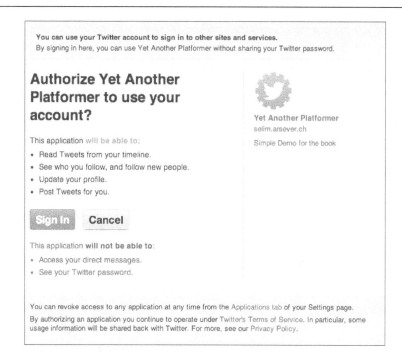

Then, once the player does this, he/she will be redirected back to the URL you specified in the `callback.php` file. If the player has already done this once, he/she will just be able to log in directly.

What would be useful from now on is the ability to know in our JavaScript code whether a player is already connected or not. To do this, let's transform our game HTML file into a PHP file and add the following code at its beginning:

```php
<?php
session_start();

require_once('twitter/twitteroauth/twitteroauth.php');
require_once('twitter/config.php');

/* Get user access tokens out of the session. */
$access_token = $_SESSION['access_token'];
$connection = new TwitterOAuth(CONSUMER_KEY, CONSUMER_SECRET, $access_token['oauth_token'], $access_token['oauth_token_secret']);
$user = $connection->get('account/verify_credentials');

?>
```

This code enables session tracking, includes some files of the `twitteroauth` library, and then checks to see if an access token is stored in the session. This will be the case if the player logged in with Twitter.

Then, the server connects to Twitter to retrieve the user object. This is all well and good, but the JavaScript code still has no idea about all this. What we need for this is to create a custom script with the values we want to transmit to the client's JavaScript:

```
<script type="text/javascript">
<?php if($_SESSION['status'] == 'verified'){ ?>
  var twitter = true;
  var twitterName = "<?php print $user->screen_name; ?>";
<?php } else { ?>
  var twitter = false;
<?php } ?>
</script>
```

Now, if the player is logged in with Twitter, we will have the global variable `twitter` set to `true` and the global variable `twitterName` holding the player's screen name.

One last thing that you may want to do is to give feedback to the user that he/she is successfully logged in with Twitter and give him/her the possibility to log out. To do this, we will slightly change the start screen if the player is already logged in:

```
<div id="startScreen" class="screen">
  <?php if($_SESSION['status'] != 'verified'){ ?>
    <a class="button tweetLink" href="./twitter/redirect.php">Login
with Twitter</a>
  <?php } else { ?>
    <a class="button tweetLink" href="./twitter/clearsessions.
php">Logout from Twitter</a>
  <?php }?>
  <a id="startButton"class="button" href="#">Start game</a>
</div>
```

With these relatively small changes, you've already implemented authentication through Twitter.

Publishing high scores on Twitter

Now that the user is connected to Twitter, you can allow him/her to tweet his/her time in a much more seamless manner. To do this, we will create a new server-side script called `twitterPost.php`. This file will use Twitter's `statuses/update` API.

Let's have a look at the complete script:

```php
<?php
session_start();
require_once('twitter/twitteroauth/twitteroauth.php');
require_once('twitter/config.php');

$time = $_SESSION['time'];
$level = $_SESSION['level'];
if(isset($time) && isset($level)){
  /* Get user access tokens out of the session. */
  $access_token = $_SESSION['access_token'];
  $connection = new TwitterOAuth(CONSUMER_KEY, CONSUMER_SECRET,
$access_token['oauth_token'], $access_token['oauth_token_secret']);

  $parameters = array('status' => 'I\'ve just finished level
'.$level.' for Yet Another Platformer in '.$time.' seconds!');
  $status = $connection->post('statuses/update', $parameters);
}
?>
```

You probably recognized most of the code from what we added at the beginning of our game page (only the highlighted part is new). The last two lines create and then send to Twitter the status you want to publish. It's pretty straightforward, but there is more to what we can do—since the player is logged in, you know his/her screen name, which you can use for the leaderboard.

In the client-side code, we will generate a slightly different version of the leaderboard as follows:

```javascript
$.ajax({
  dataType: "json",
  url: "highscore.php",
  data: {
    // ...
  },
  async: false,
  success: function (json) {
    var top = "";
    for (var i = 0; i < json.top.length; i++){
      if(json.intop && json.pos === i){
        if (twitter){
          top += "<input id='name' type='hidden'
val='"+twitterName+"'/>"
```

```
            + twitterName + " " + minSec(json.top[i].time)
            + " <a id='saveScore' href='#'>submit</a>"
            + " <a id='tweetScore' href='#'>tweet</a> <br>";
        } else {
            top += "<input id='name' placeholder='_____' size='5' />"
            + " "+minSec(json.top[i].time)
            + " <a id='saveScore' href='#'>submit</a>"
            + " <a target='_blank' href='http://twitter.com/
home?status="+escape("I've just finished level "+currentLevel+" in YAP
in "+minSec(json.top[i].time)+"!")+"'>tweet</a> <br>";
        }
    } else {
        top += "" + json.top[i].name + " " + minSec(json.top[i].time)
+ "<br>";
        }
    }
    $("#top_list").html(top);
    }
});
```

Here, we make the input field holding the player's name hidden and fill it with the user's screen name. Then, we write the screen name in the leaderboard. The nice thing with this is that the server-side code doesn't change at all.

That's all that we will implement with Twitter here, but I encourage you to take a look at the complete Twitter API and be creative!

Integrating with Facebook

In many ways, integration with Facebook resembles integration with Twitter. Facebook offers, however, much more game orientation. In our case, we will implement achievements for logged-in users. We will use Facebook's PHP SDK, but other languages are supported too.

As for Twitter, we need to first register our application in Facebook. To do this, log in to Facebook's developer website (https://developers.facebook.com/) and click on **Apps** in the header:

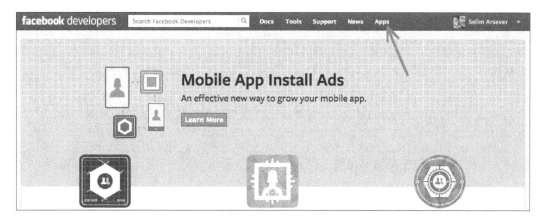

Then, click on **Create New Apps** and fill in the required information. You will then be prompted with your newly created application page. Here, you'll have to note the two values shown in the following screenshot (just as we did for Twitter):

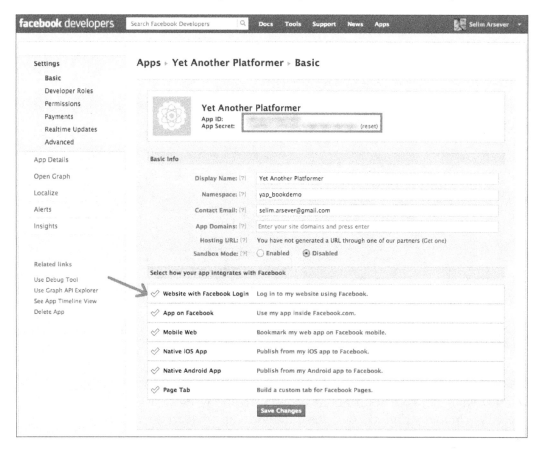

If you look at the red arrow in the preceding screenshot, you'll notice that you can choose how your app and Facebook will interact. To have full access to Facebook's Open Graph API that allows you, amongst other things, to publish achievements, you need to select **App on Facebook**.

This will allow you to have your game load into an iframe in Facebook itself. To do this, you will, however, need to have a valid HTTPS certificate installed on your domain name. But if you only want your game to load from your own server, then you don't need any (you'll still need to enter an address in the corresponding field, and you can simply prefix your non-secure address with `https` to make it valid).

There is one last step that you need to take to make it possible for your Facebook application to give achievements—register it as a game. To do this, simply click on **App Details** on the left. Then, select **Games** under **App Info | Category**, as shown in the following screenshot:

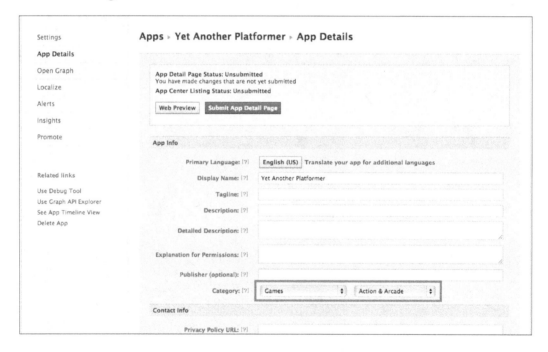

Authenticating with Facebook

The basic authentication mechanism for Facebook is very similar to that of Twitter. There is, however, a small difference with regard to the access—in Twitter, you had to define that your application needed read and write access in the developer's website, whereas with Facebook, the granularity of what access you ask the user for is much finer and it's only during the login phase that you specify those.

Let's have a look at the code required for authentication. Just as for Twitter, we will first write the instructions that try to get the user at the beginning of our game file:

```php
<?php
session_start();


// Twitter ...

// Facebook
require 'facebook/facebook.php';

$app_id = '(1)';
$app_secret = '(2)';
$app_namespace = 'yap_bookdemo';
$app_url = 'http://yetanotherplatformer.com/';
$scope = 'publish_actions';

$facebook = new Facebook(array(
   'appId' => $app_id,
   'secret' => $app_secret,
));

// Get the current user
$facebookUser = $facebook->getUser();

?>
```

The highlighted line defines that we want our game to be able to publish entries on the player's timeline. The values, (1) and (2), are the values that you noted in the application configuration page.

If $facebookUser is null, it means that the user is already logged in, otherwise we will have to display a login button. To do this, we will write a code very similar to the one we wrote for Twitter:

```php
<div id="startScreen" class="screen">
   ...
   <?php if(!$facebookUser){
     $loginUrl = $facebook->getLoginUrl(array(
       'scope' => $scope,
       'redirect_uri' => $app_url
     ));
   ?>
```

```
      <a class="button tweetLink" href="<?php print $loginUrl; ?>">Login
with Facebook</a>
    <?php } else {
      $logoutUrl = $facebook->getLogoutUrl(array(
        'next' => $app_url
      ));
    ?>
      <a class="button tweetLink" href="<?php print $logoutUrl;
?>">Logout from Facebook</a>
    <?php } ?>
    <a id="startButton"class="button" href="#">Start game</a>
  </div>
```

Here, you can see that Facebook's PHP SDK offers a convenient method to generate the URL for logging the user in or out.

Now, we will add a small piece of code to indicate to the JavaScript code whether the user is logged in to Facebook or not. Once again, the code here is very similar to the code we used for Twitter:

```
<script type="text/javascript">
  // ...
  <?php if($facebookUser){ ?>
    var facebook = true;
    var facebookId = "<?php print $facebookUser; ?>";
  <?php } else { ?>
    var facebook = false;
  <?php } ?>
</script>
```

Creating achievements

We will now create an achievement for our game. To do so, you will need two files on your server:

- An HTML file with a series of meta tags in the header
- An image file that will represent the achievement in the player's timeline

The HTML file will not only serve as a configuration file for your achievement, but it will also be linked to the achievement publication on your player's timeline. For Facebook to recognize the achievement as valid, you need to have the following seven meta tags defined in the header:

- og:type contains the value game.achievement. It differentiates achievements from other kinds of OpenGraph entities.

- `og:title` is a very short description of the achievement.
- `og:url` is the URL of the current file.
- `og:description` is a longer description of the achievement.
- `og:image` is the image mentioned earlier. It can be in PNG, JPEG, or GIF format and have a minimum size of 50 x 50 pixels. The maximum aspect ratio is 3:1.
- `game:points` is the number of points associated with this achievement. In total, your game cannot give more than 1000 points and the smallest number allowed is 1. Achievements with greater point values will have a higher probability to be displayed on the player's friend's news feed.
- `fb:app_id` is your application's ID.

The body of the HTML file can be a nice page explaining what this achievement is all about, or anything you really want. A very simple example of a complete achievement page is as follows:

```html
<html>
  <head>
    <meta property="og:type" content="game.achievement" />
    <meta property="og:title" content="Finished level 1" />
    <meta property="og:url" content="http://8bitentropy.com/yap/ach1.
html" />
    <meta property="og:description" content="You just finished the
first level!" />
    <meta property="og:image" content="http://8bitentropy.com/yap/
ach1.png" />
    <meta property="game:points" content="50" />
    <meta property="fb:app_id" content="(1)" />
  </head>
  <body>
    <h1>Well done, you finished level 1!</h1>
  </body>
</html>
```

The resulting achievement will appear similar to the following screenshot on the player's timeline:

But, writing this document is not enough for your achievement to be completely configured. You will have to submit it to Facebook. To do this, you have to do a POST request at the correct URL with the correct parameters. This request should also be associated with an application token.

Application tokens are a way in which Facebook ensures that it's really your game and not some other application that is communicating with it. The easiest way to do this is to write a PHP page that will in turn submit your achievement(s). Here is the complete code:

```php
<?php

require 'facebook/facebook.php';

$app_id = '(1)';
$app_secret = '(2)';
$app_namespace = 'yap_bookdemo';
$app_url = 'http://yetanotherplatformer.com/';
$scope = 'publish_actions';

$facebook = new Facebook(array(
  'appId' => $app_id,
  'secret' => $app_secret,
));

$app_access_token = get_app_access_token($app_id, $app_secret);
$facebook->setAccessToken($app_access_token);

$response = $facebook->api('/(1)/achievements', 'post', array(
  'achievement' => 'http://yetanotherplatformer.com//ach1.html',
));

print($response);

// Helper function to get an APP ACCESS TOKEN
function get_app_access_token($app_id, $app_secret) {
    $token_url = 'https://graph.facebook.com/oauth/access_token?'
      . 'client_id=' . $app_id
      . '&client_secret=' . $app_secret
      . '&grant_type=client_credentials';

    $token_response =file_get_contents($token_url);
    $params = null;
    parse_str($token_response, $params);
```

Chapter 8

```
        return $params['access_token'];
    }


    ?>
```

This code is quite verbose, but you'll recognize most of it from the previous ones. The important part has been highlighted—first, we retrieve the application token, then we associate it with the future request, and finally we use the SDK to do the POST request.

The address for this POST request is formatted as follows: "Application ID" / "achievements". The transmitted parameter is simply the URL of the achievement file.

Since the error message generated here (if something goes wrong) can be quite obscure, you may want to first validate your achievement file by using the debugging tool provided by Facebook at `https://developers.facebook.com/tools/debug/`.

Publishing the achievements

Now that Facebook has registered the achievement, we can award it to our players. The command to do this is also a POST request and must also be associated with an application token. For the sake of simplicity, we will create a simple PHP page that will award the achievement when called. This is far from optimal in a real-life situation, where you want to avoid having the user simply call the file himself/ herself. You can award the achievement in the `highscore.php` file instead.

This is the complete code of this file; it is very similar to the file we used to register our achievements, and the differences are highlighted:

```php
<?php
session_start();

// Facebook
require 'facebook/facebook.php';

$app_id = '(1)';
$app_secret = '(2)';
$app_namespace = 'yap_bookdemo';
$app_url = 'http://yetanotherplatformer.com/';
$scope = 'publish_actions';

$facebook = new Facebook(array(
    'appId' => $app_id,
    'secret' => $app_secret,
```

[173]

```
));

// Get the current user
$facebookUser = $facebook->getUser();

$app_access_token = get_app_access_token($app_id, $app_secret);
$facebook->setAccessToken($app_access_token);

$response = $facebook->api('/'.$facebookUser.'/achievements', 'post',
array(
  'achievement' => 'http://yetanotherplatformer.com/ach1.html'
));

print($response);

// Helper function to get an APP ACCESS TOKEN
function get_app_access_token($app_id, $app_secret) {
  ...
}


?>
```

This time, we create a POST request to a URL with the format: "User ID" / "achievements". Now, we simply have to asynchronously call this file from our game when the user finishes the first level:

```
if (status == "finished") {
  ...
  if(facebook && currentLevel === 1){
    $.get("ac h1.php");
  }
  ...
```

Summary

We've learned a lot during this chapter, even though we have only scratched the surface of what kind of social interactions are possible with the new tools. Facebook and Twitter's APIs are large and change constantly. If you want to use them in the best possible way, I would really recommend reading their complete documentation.

But, when using third-party services, especially the free ones, you have to realize that you become dependent on them. They can change anything at any time, without giving you much notice. They can decide that they don't want your game to use their service anymore. Always keep this in mind, and if possible, make sure that you have an exit strategy in those situations!

In the next chapter, we will explore another hot topic — making your game mobile! For this, we will take our platformer and expand it to work on modern smartphones and tablets.

Making Your Game Mobile

9

Mobile devices are quickly becoming the go-to platform for gaming. The good news is that the web browsers in most of these devices are pretty good, and in most cases, you can make your mobile game run smoothly on them.

These devices have, however, some memory and power limitations. There are some games that simply won't work on a mobile browser at the moment. You cannot expect to have just as many sprites running smoothly on your smartphone that has one-tenth of the power of your desktop computer.

On the plus side, a mobile device offers a few capabilities you typically don't find on a desktop:

- The multi-touch interface allows for new kinds of interaction with your game
- The device orientation API allows you to control your game or UI in interesting ways
- Most devices allow your game to be installed to the "springboard" just like a native app, blurring the line between browser games and native ones
- An offline cache allows your game to work even without an Internet connection active on the device

In this chapter, we will take our MMORP and make it work on an iOS device. Most of the APIs we will use are de facto standards and are supported on Android as well. Here is a short overview of the topics we will cover:

- Dealing with the performance limitations of mobile devices
- Adding multi-touch control to our game
- Integrating our game with the springboard and other mobile-specific configuration
- Using the device orientation API
- Taking advantage of web storage and the offline application cache

We chose to only consider the iOS side of things for several reasons:

- iOS is still globally the most commonly used mobile OS even though Android has caught up recently (depending on the source and what exactly is considered a mobile device, you will find market share for iOS between 30 percent and 50 percent).

- Even if the choice Apple made to forbid a third-party browser for its OS has been very controversial, it has the positive side effect of making web development much easier. Indeed, you don't have to deal with too much diversity on the browser side.

- Most of the specific APIs available on mobile browsers have first been created or implemented by Apple on Webkit mobile.

Before we begin, I'd like to emphasize the fact that this is a field that evolves even faster than the rest of the web development world. New APIs are regularly added and the performance of each new device is significantly better than the one it replaces. If you are serious about making games that take full advantage of mobile devices, you should invest some time to keep yourself up-to-date with those changes.

Making your game run well on mobile devices

Performance issues are probably the single biggest problem you will encounter when developing a browser-based mobile game, the main reason being that a wide variety of devices is available, each with very different capabilities.

Even if you chose to support only iOS, which is probably the simplest ecosystem at the moment, you will still have very large differences in performance, screen resolution, and browser support.

To get an idea of the complexity of the situation, take a look at the supported device for jQuery Mobile (`http://jquerymobile.com/gbs/`). For your game, you should probably have an approach similar to theirs; select a few device/software versions you will target. Your game should work flawlessly on those.

Then make sure that the game runs without errors on a broader selection of devices. On those devices, performance can be less than ideal. Finally, draw a clear line beyond which you won't even bother to test whether your game runs at all.

The size of each of these categories will depend on how much effort you want to invest in them. One problem is that you can't really use the emulators provided with each platform's SDK to investigate performance issues. This means that, in the end, you will have to test your game on actual devices.

This is not a problem for large companies, but if you are a small indie game developer, you will probably find this to be a limiting factor on the number of devices you will support.

Detecting mobile browsers

To cope with the differences between the desktop and the mobile device there are many possible approaches:

1. Design one game only with mobile devices in mind. It will run without any problem on desktops too but may not be as beautiful or as complex as it might have been had it been designed specifically for desktops. The good thing is that if players compete with one another in your game, they will all be on the same level.

2. Design two games, one optimized for desktop and one for mobile. This is almost twice the work, but you will probably share a big part of the art, music, and server-side code (if any). This is the ideal solution in terms of performances, but if you have PvP (player versus player) in your game player on one platform, it could be advantageous compared to those in the other platforms.

3. You could design only one game but add some purely cosmetic features if the game runs on a desktop browser. With this solution, you have only one code base, but it may be slightly more complex. The problem with the PvP game remains.

The approach you will choose to follow will depend on your priorities, but for the second and third approaches, you will need to detect what kind of platform the player is running your game on.

Depending on how precise you want to be, this can be quite a complex task. There are basically two general methods you can use: client-side detecting and server-side detecting.

Client-side browser detection

If what you want is to implement the third approach described previously, detecting the browser on the client side makes a lot of sense. The most common approach is to use the `navigator.userAgent` string (**UA** for short). This variable contains a very long and cryptic string that holds a lot of information.

It's important to keep in mind that the browser can fake this string (this is called **UA spoofing**). For example, in Safari, you can specify which browser it should imitate. The good thing is that mobile devices typically don't offer this without some hacking on the user part. Furthermore, some very different mobiles have the same UA such as the desktop and mobile versions of Internet Explorer.

A big part of it is here for legacy reasons, and you really shouldn't bother with it, but by looking at the occurrence of a given string in this longer string, you can detect what kind of browser you're dealing with. For example, if the `userAgent` string contains `iPhone`, you know that the browser is Safari mobile running on an iPhone. The corresponding JavaScript would be something like this:

```
if (navigator.userAgent.match(/iPhone/i)) {
    // iPhone detected
    // ...
} else {
    // not an iPhone
}
```

Now this will work for an iPhone, but if your user is using an iPad, it won't be detected. You have to look for the string `iPad` to detect an iPad. The same goes for iPod Touch, where you would have to look for `iPod`. If you want to differentiate between iDevices and others, you could do something like this:

```
if (navigator.userAgent.match(/iPhone|iPod|iPad/i)) {
    // iDevice detected
    // ...
} else {
    // not an iDevice
}
```

If you want the granularity to detect individual devices, you should use the following code:

```
if (navigator.userAgent.match(/iPhone/i)) {
    // iPhone detected
} else if (navigator.userAgent.match(/iPad/i)) {
    // iPad detected
```

```
} else if(navigator.userAgent.match(/iPod/i)) {
  // iPod touch detected
} else {
    // not an iDevice
}
```

As you can imagine, this list could quickly become quite long if you want to detect a large number of devices. Hopefully, there exist code snippets that do exactly what you are aiming to do. If you just want to detect mobile devices, you can use the script provided at `http://detectmobilebrowsers.com/`. If you want more control of what exactly it is that you detect, you can use the script provided by the always excellent Peter-Paul Koch at `http://www.quirksmode.org/js/detect.html`.

Server-side detection

If what you want is to implement the second approach (different versions of your game for mobile and desktop browsers), you will probably want to detect the player's browser on the server and redirect them to the right version of the game. As with client-side detection, the most common technique uses the browser's `userAgent` string.

If you use PHP, you will be happy to learn that it almost supports browser detection out of the box. Indeed, you can use the `get_browser` function in conjunction with an up-to-date `php_browscap.ini` file to get information about the browser (you can find various versions of this file at `http://tempdownloads.browserscap.com/`). You will have to configure the `browscap` property in your `php.ini` file to point to your `php_browscap.ini` file for it to be recognized. The code to replicate the client-side detection we've implemented previously would look like this:

```
$browser = get_browser(null);

if($browser->platform == "iOS"){
  echo "iOS";
} else {
  echo "not iOS";
}
```

This has the same shortcoming as the client-side implementation: the browser can forge the `userAgent` string.

Should you really detect the browser?

It's not generally considered good practice to detect the browser. The preferred solution is generally to use feature detection. For example, this really makes sense if you want to use device orientation, then you will simply check if the corresponding API is available at runtime.

In this situation, it is a far more robust approach, but what we're talking about here is optimizing the game performance-wise. There is no feature that you can detect that will provide information about this. In this situation, I would argue that browser detection makes sense.

A more robust alternative would be to run a very quick benchmark before starting the game to extrapolate the performance of the device your game is running on. This would be a lot of work but can be worth the effort in situations where you can scale the performance of your game linearly. For example, you could define the number of trees you use to draw a forest in a very fine way, say, 80 percent of the maximum number of trees.

This is typically the case if you use a lot of particle effects. Then it's very easy to change the total number of particles you use to match the device performance.

Performance limitation – memory

Now that we're able to detect that the game runs on a mobile device, we will be able to adapt to the device's limitations. The first thing that probably pops up in your mind when talking about performance is the speed of the processor, but most of the time, memory is a bigger limitation.

On the desktop, you don't need to think about memory anymore, in most cases (except to avoid memory leaks). On mobile devices, memory is a much more limited resource, and sometimes, simply loading a big image is too much for the browser. For example, the maximum allowed size for an image is as follows for iDevices:

	< 256 MB of RAM	> 256 MB of RAM
GIF, PNG, and TIFF images	3 megapixels	5 megapixels
JPEG	32 megapixels	32 megapixels
Canvas DOM element	3 megapixels	5 megapixels

It's important to note that this has absolutely nothing to do with the compression of the image. Indeed, though it's important to compress your images to reduce the time it will take to download them for the memory imprint, the only thing that matters is the resolution.

So if compression isn't going to help, what can we do? Let's take the example of our multiplayer RPG. There, we used a very large image with all the tiles for our tile map. Many of those tiles are not actually used in the map we created for our game. So, a very simple way to reduce this very large image is to remove all the tiles we don't need.

This means that instead of having one large image that you will use through the whole game, you will have a smaller image for each zone. This will increase the complexity of the code because it means managing the transition between zones, but it has the advantage of not degrading your level design at all.

In some situations, even with this technique you will find it hard to reduce the size of the image enough. One easy solution is to have two versions of the level, one for the desktop and the other for mobile platforms. On the mobile version, you will reduce the variety of tiles. For example, in our game we use multiple tiles to render grass, as shown in the following figure:

Here, we could simply use a single tile instead. Sure, the resulting graphics will be less varied, but it will dramatically decrease the number of tiles you'll need. This has, however, the disadvantage of requiring you to maintain two separate versions of each level.

Performance limitation – speed

The performance for mobile devices varies greatly, but even the fastest ones are still way slower than any desktop. This means that there are games that simply won't run on mobile devices, no matter how much effort you put into them. There are, however, many games that you can slightly transform to make them run at a reasonable speed.

When making a DOM-based game, there are not many areas where you can speed things up. The first thing you should do is to try reducing the number of sprites or tiles.

Specifying the page's visible area

A very simple way to reduce the number of tiles is to make the game area smaller. You may think this is a very bad idea since what you really want is for the game area to fill up the entire screen, which means adapting to the device resolution. Well, yes...and no! Yes, you want the game area to fill the entire screen, but no, that doesn't necessarily mean using the full resolution.

Mobile browsers offer a very handy `meta` property that allows you to specify how the browser should manage the page width. This will come in handy here since we can basically choose the size you want for the game area and then force the browser to display it in fullscreen mode.

This property is called viewport, and to specify a given width for the screen you can simply write:

```
<meta name="viewport" content="user-scalable=no, width=480" />
```

We configure two different behaviors here. First, we say to the browser that the original width of the page is 480 pixels. Let's say the device's native resolution is 960 pixels; this will mean that the page will be zoomed in to. Had the device resolution been 320 pixels, the page would have been zoomed out of.

The second thing we do here is to disable the zoom function for the user. This is not necessary if you want to use touch events later; to control the game, you want to be sure that the user won't zoom in or out while trying to manipulate the game.

Level of details

Reducing the number of sprites can be tricky. For example, you don't want to reduce the number of NPCs (Non Player Characters) or enemies in the game. Identifying the element that can be removed is a tedious task.

The following figure is taken from *Chapter 5, Putting Things into Perspective*. It's a quick reminder of the structure of the tile map we used for our RPG.

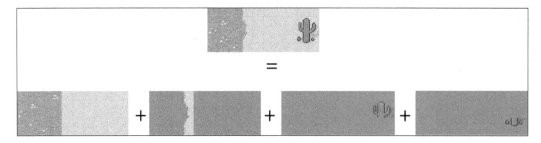

If you keep the purely decorative elements in the last two layers in this figure it becomes easy to reduce the number of sprites; if needed, just delete those two layers and you're done.

It doesn't necessarily mean that you have to get rid of all those elements. What you could do is have two different versions of those layers, one with a lot of elements and one with way fewer.

If you really need to reduce the number of sprites even further, you will have to consider the impact it will have on the gameplay. There is no standard answer here; you will have to approach each game individually and find the right balance between keeping your gameplay like you originally intended the and speed of your game.

Touch control

Until now we've only talked about the problematic parts of mobile devices, but there are also advantages that come with these devices. Touch screens allow for a very interesting game mechanism (and multi-touch screens even more so).

In this section, we will implement two different ways of controlling our game with touches, but it's really a field where you can be creative and find novel and engaging ways for the player to interact with your game. What is important to know is that the API for touch control is not standard, and mobile devices may implement it with some differences. Nevertheless, the code shown in the following section should work on iOS and on recent versions of Android.

Both interfaces we will implement are based on the same basic idea: the whole screen is a joypad, and no visible UI elements are used. The advantage of this is that the bigger the surface used for control, the more precise the control. The disadvantage is that you need to explain to the user how it works if he/she will not be able to discover it by himself/herself by simply looking at the screen.

The code we use can easily be adapted to work with smaller control placed at the bottom/side of the screen.

D-pad

A d-pad (short for directional pad) is a kind of control that was used in old-school game consoles. It provides a few predefined directions the user can choose between (for example, up, down, left, and right). By contrast, joysticks provide an analogic interface, where the player can choose a precise direction (for example, a 30 degree angle). The first control methods we will implement divide the screen into five zones as shown in the following figure:

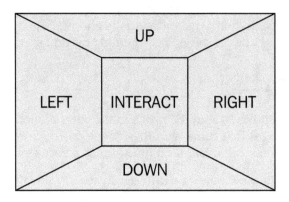

The advantage is that this method has a one-to-one mapping with the keyboard control. If the player touches the **UP** zone, it will correspond to pressing the up arrow on the keyboard and so on for the other border zones. If the player touches the center zone, it will correspond to pressing the Space bar.

To implement this, we will create five virtual keys and expand the part of the code that checks for keyboard input to check for that as well. The following code extract is the definition of those virtual keys:

```
var UP = {
  on: false,
  id: 0
};
var DOWN = {
  on: false,
  id: 0
};
var LEFT = {
  on: false,
  id: 0
};
var RIGHT ={
```

```
    on: false,
    id: 0
  };
  var INTERACT ={
    on: false,
    id: 0
  };
```

As you can see, those keys have ID fields. This is necessary because we are dealing with multi-touch events, and we have to be able to identify which touch events ended to turn the on field back to false when the player lifts his/her finger.

To detect that the player touches the screen, we will register a touchstart event handler. This event is similar to the onmousedown event, except that it contains a list of touches. This makes sense because we're dealing with multi-touch input and we cannot simply assume that only one finger is touching the screen.

All those touches are stored in the event.changedTouches array. In your event handler, you simply need to look at each of them. The following code extract is the whole event handler:

```
document.addEventListener('touchstart', function(e) {
  if(gameStarted){
    e.preventDefault();
    for (var i = 0; i < e.changedTouches.length; i++){
      var touch = e.changedTouches[i]

      var x = touch.pageX - 480 / 2;
      var y = touch.pageY - 320 / 2;

      if (Math.abs(x) < 20 && Math.abs(y) < 20){
        INTERACT.on = true;
        INTERACT.id = touch.identifier;

      } else if (Math.abs(x) > 480 / 320 *  Math.abs(y)) {
        // left or right
        if(x > 0){
          RIGHT.on = true;
          RIGHT.id = touch.identifier;
        } else {
          LEFT.on = true;
          LEFT.id = touch.identifier;
        }
      } else {
        // up or down
```

```
          if(y > 0){
            DOWN.on = true;
            DOWN.id = touch.identifier;
          } else {
            UP.on = true;
            UP.id = touch.identifier;
          }
        }
      }
    }
  }, false);
```

Since "jQuery Core" doesn't support touch events, we use the standard way to register event handlers. Then we prevent the events from bubbling up to make sure they won't produce zooms, scroll, and so on. The last part of this event handler checks for each touch to find out what zone it's on, switches the on flag of the corresponding key to `true`, and sets the correct `id` value for tracking.

Now we need to be able to detect when the touch ends. This is done with `touchend` event. This event works in a similar way to the `touchstart` one, and the code of the event handler has the same structure. Here we don't need to worry about the position of the touch but only about its ID. We will then switch the on flag of the corresponding touch back to `false`.

```
document.addEventListener('touchend', function(e) {
  if(gameStarted){
    e.preventDefault();

    for (var i = 0; i < e.changedTouches.length; i++){
        var touch = e.changedTouches[i]
        if (touch.identifier === UP.id){
         UP.on = false;
        }
        if (touch.identifier === LEFT.id){
         LEFT.on = false;
        }
        if (touch.identifier === RIGHT.id){
         RIGHT.on = false;
        }
        if (touch.identifier === DOWN.id){
         DOWN.on = false;
        }
```

```
            if (touch.identifier === INTERACT.id){
              INTERACT.on = false;
            }
          }
        }
      }, false);
```

Now that our virtual keys hold the correct value, we can use them in our code as we used the array that holds the state of the real keys. That's exactly what the following code does; the modified parts have been highlighted:

```
var gameLoop = function() {
    var idle = true;

    if(gf.keyboard[37] || LEFT.on){ //left arrow
        player.left();
     idle = false;
    }
    if(gf.keyboard[38] || UP.on){ //up arrow
     player.up();
     idle = false;
    }
    if(gf.keyboard[39] || RIGHT.on){ //right arrow
        player.right();
        idle = false;
    }
    if(gf.keyboard[40] || DOWN.on){ //down arrow
     player.down();
     idle = false;
    }
    if(gf.keyboard[32] || INTERACT.on){ //space
        player.strike();
        idle = false;
    }
    if(idle){
        player.idle();
    }

    // ...
};
```

With these simple modifications, we've implemented the first version of our touch control.

Analog joystick

The previous control method was fine, but you may want to allow the player a more natural way to make the avatar move. This is where the following method comes in. Here, we only have two zones: a small one in the center that works like the Space bar and the rest of the screen. The following figure shows these two zones:

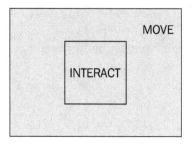

If the player touches this bigger zone, the avatar will move in the direction of the touch. If the fingers of the player change direction, the avatar's movement will change accordingly, as shown in the following figure:

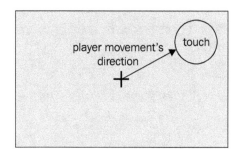

To implement this means slightly changing the way the player is controlled, so we've added a new method to the `player` object: `direction`. This function takes an angle in degrees and extrapolates the most appropriate animation as well as the new position of the player. The following code shows this function:

```
this.move = function(angle){
  if(state !== "strike"){
    var xratio = Math.cos(angle);
    var yratio = Math.sin(angle);
    if(Math.abs(xratio) > Math.abs(yratio)){
      if(xratio < 0){
        this.left();
      } else {
```

```
        this.right();
      }
    } else {
      if (yratio < 0){
        this.up();
      } else {
        this.down();
      }
    }
    moveX = 3*xratio;
    moveY = 3*yratio;
    }
  };
```

There is only one piece of code worth pointing out here, highlighted in the preceding snippet. To compute the vertical and horizontal movement from the angle, we use sine and cosine functions. Their meaning is explained in the following figure:

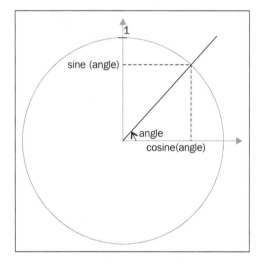

Those two functions will give us a number between -1 and 1 that represent how much the player should move along each axis. We then simply multiply this by the maximum movement (3, in our case) to get the real movement along each axis.

We do nothing to support the case where the player tries to control the game with the keyboard and the touch screen since this is very unlikely.

Event handlers

Now we will use a pattern somewhat similar to what we used before with our virtual keys. Here we will have only two of them. One will be the same as before: the interaction key. The second one is a bit special since it will be used to store the angle at which the avatar should move.

The `touchstart` event handler is almost the same as before, except that we compute the angle between the touch and the center of the screen:

```
document.addEventListener('touchstart', function(e) {
    if(gameStarted){
        for (var i = 0; i < e.changedTouches.length; i++){
            var touch = e.changedTouches[i];
            var x = touch.pageX - 480 / 2;
            var y = touch.pageY - 320 / 2;
            var radius = Math.sqrt(Math.pow(x,2)+Math.pow(y,2));

            if(radius < 30) {
                INTERACT.on = true;
                INTERACT.id = touch.identifier;
            } else if(!MOVE.on){
                MOVE.on = true;
                MOVE.id = touch.identifier;
                MOVE.angle = Math.atan2(y,x);
            }
        }
    }
}, false);
```

For this, we use another trigonometric function: cotangent. This function allows us to retrieve the angle between two segments of a right triangle as shown in the following figure:

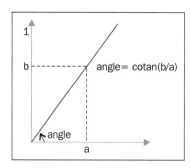

The `touchend` handler is identical to the previous one but for the two virtual keys:

```
document.addEventListener('touchend', function(e) {
  if(gameStarted){
    for (var i = 0; i < e.changedTouches.length; i++){
      var touch = e.changedTouches[i]
      if (touch.identifier === INTERACT.id){
        INTERACT.on = false;
      }
      if (touch.identifier === MOVE.id){
        MOVE.on = false;
      }
    }
  }
}, false);
```

We will need a third event handler to track the movement of the fingers between the start of the touch and its end. This handler has a structure similar to that of `touchend` but updates the angle of the MOVE virtual key:

```
document.addEventListener('touchmove', function(e) {
  if(gameStarted){
    e.preventDefault();
    for (var i = 0; i < e.changedTouches.length; i++){
      var touch = e.changedTouches[i];
      if (touch.identifier === MOVE.id){
        var x = touch.pageX - 480 / 2;
        var y = touch.pageY - 320 / 2;
        MOVE.angle = Math.atan2(y,x);
      }
    }
  }
}, false);
```

With those three event handlers, our new control interface is implemented. You really have to try them to see which one you prefer. Those methods are really only two among many others, and choosing the right one will have a big influence on the success of your game on mobile devices, so don't hesitate to try a lot of them before choosing the final one!

Integrating our game with the springboard

There is a very elegant way to make your game run in fullscreen mode on iOS. With the proper configuration, we can make your game installable on the springboard. This will have several effects: the game will run without any browser UI element, and it will have an icon and a splash screen.

All this is done through setting a series of `meta` tags in the document header.

Making your game installable

To make your game installable you have to use the `apple-mobile-web-app-capable` `meta` tag in your document head with the value `yes`. Once this is done the player will be able to add the game to the springboard from Safari as shown in the following screenshot:

The code you should have in your header is as follows:

```
<meta name="apple-mobile-web-app-capable" content="yes" />
```

A web page installed this way will be run without any visible browser UI elements (also called Chrome). The following figure gives the name of all the UI elements:

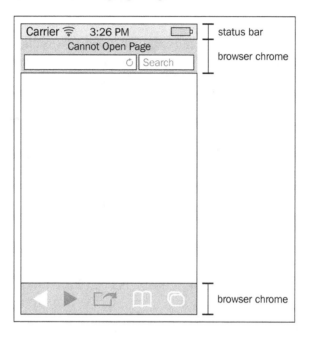

Sadly, at the time of writing, this property is not well supported by Android phones. Some of them will make the web page installable to the main screen with a custom icon but won't accept the chromeless mode. Others will simply ignore it entirely.

Configuring the status bar

Once launched from the springboard, the only remaining UI element is the status bar. As shown in the preceding figure, it's the bar at the top of the screen that holds information such as network reception and name, and remaining battery.

You can choose how this status bar looks like to make it fit your application as much as possible. This is done with the `apple-mobile-web-app-status-bar-style` `meta` tag.

The following list holds the possible values you can give to this tag and their corresponding effects:

- `default`: If you don't use this `meta` tag or give it this value, you will leave the choice of the appearance of the status bar to the OS.
- `black`: With this value, the status bar will have a black background and white text.
- `black-translucent`: With this value, the status bar will have a slightly transparent black background with white text. This setting has the peculiarity that the web page will be rendered under the status bar. This has the advantage of giving the full device resolution to the game; whereas, with the other settings, the web page will lose a few pixels on top of the screen.

The code you should have in your header is as follows:

```
<meta name="apple-mobile-web-app-status-bar-style" content="black-translucent" />
```

Specifying the application icon

If you don't specify anything, iOS will use a screenshot of the web page as an icon. If you want to specify an icon to be used instead, you will need to use one or more `link` tags. The problem is that different iDevices need different icon sizes. The solution is to specify the size of the icon in the `link` tag like this:

```
<link rel="apple-touch-icon" sizes="72x72" href="icon.png" />
```

The possible sizes are: 57 x 57, 72 x 72, 114 x 114, and 144 x 144. The icon you specified with this tag will be overlaid with a sort of gloss effect. If you want your icon to be used as is, you can use the `rel` tag `apple-touch-icon-precomposed` instead.

Specifying a splash screen

When the user launches the game, a screenshot will be displayed during the loading of the page. If you instead want to specify an image, you can use a `link` tag with the `rel` tag `apple-touch-startup-image`.

We will have the same problem as with the icon: each device has another screen resolution and should use a corresponding image. However, the way to specify the resolution of the image is different from that for the icon. Here, you will need to use the `media` attribute.

With the `media` attribute, you can specify the device width with `device-width`, the device orientation with `orientation`, and whether the device uses retina display with `-webkit-device-pixel-ratio`. A complete example would be as follows:

```
<link href="startup-image.png" media="(device-width: 320px) and
(orientation: portrait) and (-webkit-device-pixel-ratio: 2)"
rel="apple-touch-startup-image">
```

Using device orientation

In some situations, it can be useful to have access to the device orientation. For example, you can use it to control the avatar's movement. To do this, you can simply register an event handler that will receive an event each time the device orientation changes. The following code does exactly that:

```
if(window.DeviceOrientationEvent) {
  window.addEventListener("deviceorientation", function(event){
    var alpha = event.alpha;
    var beta = event.beta;
    var gamma = event.gamma;
    // do something with the orientation
  }, false);
}
```

The first `if` statement is there to check whether the device supports the device orientation API. Then we register an event handler that accesses the orientation of the device. This orientation is provided by three angles: `alpha` is the rotation around the z axis, `beta` is the rotation around the x axis, and `gamma` is the rotation around the y axis.

You already know what the x and y axes are; they are the same that we used to position the elements of our games. The z axis is an axis that points out of the screen towards the player.

The following figure shows those axes and their corresponding angles:

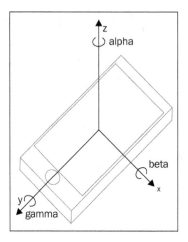

Using the offline application cache

One very useful feature of mobile devices is the ability for the web pages to work offline. For a game like the platformer we created earlier, it means that, once installed, you won't ever need a network connection again to load the game assets.

To enable offline mode, you will need to create a file called a manifest. The manifest is a list of all the files required by the game. They will be stored locally on the device during game installation on the springboard.

The format of this manifest is as follows:

```
CACHE MANIFEST

CACHE:
tilesheet.png
level.json
gameFramework.js
rpg.js
jquery.js

NETWORK:
*
```

The CACHE section lists all the files to be stored locally. The NETWORK section lists all the external resources that are accessible when the application is online. If you don't want to restrict the network access you may simply write * as in the preceding example.

To link the manifest to your game, you will use the following attribute for your html tag:

```
<html manifest="pathto/manifestFiles">
```

The manifest has to be served by the server with the MIME type text/cache-manifest.

You have to be aware that once the application is installed using such a manifest, the game's file will not be updated even if the application changed on the server. The only way to force the refreshing of the resources is to change the manifest itself. If you don't really need to change the manifest, you can simply write a version number or timestamp in a comment; this will be enough to trigger the refresh.

Another possibility is that of adding a version number on your static media. This will help avoiding some bugs in iOS where the static files are not refreshed correctly.

Using web storage

There are, however, situations where your application needs to transmit information to the server, for example, when the player hits a high score. What should you do if the game is running in offline mode at this moment?

The solution is to use web storage. We won't go into the details of all that you can do with web storage, but the basic idea here is to store all the information you want to send to the server in local storage and transmit it once the game is online again. This technology is part of the HTML5 specification and therefore supported only by modern browsers. The available space you have to save your data in is 5 MB, so you will have to use it wisely.

To store any value you want on the client's side, you can simply use the setItem method of the sessionStorage object. To retrieve the value, you can use the getItem method.

The following code shows exactly this:

```
sessionStorage.setItem('key','value');
sessionStorage.getItem('key');
```

Now if you want to check whether the game is online, you can use the `onLine` flag on the `navigator` object, as follows:

```
if (navigator.onLine) {
    // push data to the server
}
```

In the case of our RPG, you may want to store the player position and the enemies he/she killed locally and push them to the server once the Internet connection is restored.

Summary

In this chapter you've learned a lot of specific APIs and techniques available only to the mobile device. Writing games for mobile devices using web technologies is often a challenge but will greatly increase the number of potential players for your game.

You can even distribute your game in the App Store by using PhoneGap (also known as Apache Cordova).

In the next chapter we will see how to add sound and music to your game. This is a tricky thing to do with web technologies, but it's well worth the trouble!

10
Making Some Noise

This is the last chapter of this book, but it's far from the least important subject. Music and sound effects are a crucial part of a game's user experience. The right music can completely change the way a level feels. The right sound effects can help the player understand a game's mechanics or give him/her just the feedback that he/she needs to perform the right action at the right time.

Furthermore, the player expects to have sound in a game since it's been present in games since the early days of gaming. Sadly, when it comes to sound, HTML games have some big problems. There is not one single powerful solution you can use that will make it possible to add sound to your game and have it work on all browsers.

In this chapter we will cover four different techniques to add sound to your game:

- **Embedding**: This is the oldest way to include sound in a page. It was used a lot in the old days to make a page play a MIDI file as background music. It's not standard, doesn't offer a consistent JavaScript API, and you have no guarantee that a given audio format is supported. On the plus side though, it's supported by almost all the browsers you can find.

- **HTML5 Audio**: You can use the audio tag to produce sound. On the plus side, almost all browsers support it. The downside is that you will have to deal with the fact that each browser supports a different variety of codec and that you will not be able to manipulate the sound.

- **Web Audio API**: This is basically a JavaScript wrapper around OpenAL. This means that you can do anything you want with the sound. Sadly, at the moment only Chrome and Safari (on iOS too) support it.

- **Flash**: It's possible to use Flash just to play the sound. This may seem like a strange idea since we're making a JavaScript game here, but you could typically use this as a fallback for older browsers.

Then we will have a look at a few interesting tools you could use to generate sound for your game.

Abstracting audio

First let's create a very simple library to abstract interactions between our framework and the sound implementation we chose. The following code represents a "contract" that all our implementations will have to respect:

```
// a sound object
sound = function(){
  // Preloads the sound
  this.preload = function(url){
    // TODO: implement
  };

  // Returns true if the sound is preloaded
  this.isPreloaded = function(){
    // TODO: implement
  }

  // Starts to play the sound. If loop is true the
  // sound will repeat until stopped
  this.play = function(loop){
    // TODO: implement
  };

  // Stops the sound
  this.stop = function(){
    // TODO: implement
  };
};
```

For the Web Audio API implementation, we will add more capabilities to our object, but this is the basic functionality you might expect for any audio library.

Using our small library

To use a sound in our game we will simply link the corresponding implementation to our HTML file:

```
<script type="text/javascript" src="sound.js"></script>
```

Now we will add background music to our levels; we need to set up the sound and preload it. We will do this by splitting the `initialize` function into two parts:

```
var initialize = function() {
  // ...
  backgroundMusic = new sound();
```

```
      backgroundMusic.preload("background_music.mp3");
      waitForSound();
}

var waitForSound = function(){
  if (backgroundMusic.isPreloaded()){
    // ...
    backgroundMusic.play(true);
  } else {
    setTimeout(arguments.callee, 100);
  }
}
```

The waitForSound function checks whether the sound is preloaded. If it isn't, we create a timeout to check its state again later (100 milliseconds later, to be precise). As you can see, once the sound is preloaded, we start the level and play the sound. Now we need to stop the sound when the level is finished as shown in the following code:

```
var player = new (function(){
    // ...
    this.update = function () {
        if(status == "dead"){
            // ...
        } else if (status == "finished") {
            backgroundMusic.stop();
            // ...
```

Start it again when the next level begins:

```
var gameLoop = function() {
    if(gameState === "level"){
        // ..
    } else if (gameState === "menu") {

      if (gf.keyboard[32]){
        // ..
        backgroundMusic.play(true);
      }
    }
};
```

With these modifications, and if the sound library respects the contract we just specified, we will have background music. Now let's have a look at different implementations for this sound library.

Embedding sound

HTML possesses a very handy way to delegate the reading of some content to a plugin: the embed tag. It's not a standard tag but is supported by all browsers and is used widely to include Flash in websites.

This same HTML tag can be used to include sound in a web page. This is far from an ideal solution for many reasons:

- There is no standard way to know programmatically whether browsers support this feature.

- There is no standard way to control the sound playback since the exposed API depends on the plugin used to play the sound. It's possible to try to detect what plugin is loaded, but this process is not very reliable. Furthermore, it will be a lot of work to provide implementation for each possible plugin.

- The supported format depends on the plugins installed and not only on the browser.

- Even if the sound format is supported, the browser may ask permission to start the plugin. As long as the user hasn't accepted the launch of the plugin, no sound will be played.

There may be some use cases where it's reasonable to use this method to include sounds in your game, but if any of the other techniques presented in the rest of this chapter work for you, I would recommend using those instead.

Implementation

Let's have a look at the part of the implementation that takes care of the preloading:

```
// Preloads the sound
this.preload = function(url){
  // Preloading is not supported in a consistant
  // way for embeded sounds so we just save the
  // URL for later use.
  this.url = url;
};

// Returns true if the sound is preloaded
this.isPreloaded = function(){
  // Since we use no preloading we always return true
  return true;
}
```

Implementing preloading with the `embed` tag would require the knowledge of the exact plugin being used to play the sound. Sadly, this isn't possible. Instead we've chosen to create a completely generic implementation. As a side effect, we cannot support preloading. The previous code simply bypasses preloading by always returning `true`.

This creates a major problem: the file will only start to load when you want to play it. This means that there will be quite a large delay between the call to the `play` function and the time when the player hears the sound. This isn't a big issue for background music, but for sound effects it makes this time almost worthless. On the plus side, the second time you play the sound it will probably have been cached, so the delay should be reduced.

Since we don't want to use any JavaScript API to interact with the plugin, we will simply inject the `embed` tag into the page and configure it to automatically start playback.

```
// Starts to play the sound. If loop is true the
// sound will repeat until stopped
this.play = function(loop){
  var embed = "<embed width='0' height='0' src='";
  embed += this.url;
  embed += "' loop='";
  embed += (loop)? "true" : "false";
  embed += "' autostart='true' />";
  this.obj = $(embed);
  $("body").append(this.obj);
};
```

We store the generated tag in order to remove it during the `stop` method:

```
// Stops the sound
this.stop = function(){
  this.obj.remove();
};
```

The disadvantage of this is that we don't reuse the tag we've created. But as you won't use this technique in situations where you need to create lots of sound, this is not a big issue.

Supported format

Since the list of supported formats using the `embed` tag depends on the installed plugin, it's not possible to guarantee that a given file will be playable. However, if you use WAV and MIDI, you should be safe.

If you choose to use WAV files, be careful because there are many different ways the sound can be encoded in this format, and to maximize the compatibility you should use uncompressed waves.

HTML5 Audio element

In order to match Flash's multimedia capabilities, `video` and `audio` elements were added to HTML5. They both come with matching JavaScript APIs that allow you to create and manipulate the video or sound with JavaScript without needing to write to the document (just like the `Image` object allows you to load an image without having to use the `img` tag).

First let's have a quick look at what the `audio` tag looks like:

```
<audio>
    <source src="backgroundMusic.ogg" type='audio/ogg;
codecs="vorbis"'>
    <source src="backgroundMusic.mp3" type='audio/mpeg; codecs="mp3"'>
</audio>
```

As you can see here, it's possible to provide multiple sources to the `audio` tag. This is to circumvent the single biggest issue with this API: compatibility with file formats. Indeed, even though all modern browsers support the `audio` element, there is not one single audio format that you can use that will be recognized by all of them. The solution is to provide multiple formats.

This is far from ideal since it will force you to maintain multiple versions of your sound files on your server. The following table shows the compatibility of existing sound formats with current browser versions:

	MP3	AAC	WAV	Ogg Vorbis
Chrome	✓		✓	✓
Firefox			✓	✓
Internet Explorer	✓	✓		
Opera			✓	✓
Safari	✓	✓	✓	

This means that if you want to support all browsers, you'll have to provide at least two file formats. The consensus is that you should choose MP3 and Ogg Vorbis (sound files ending with .ogg).

For a game, you typically won't use an HTML tag but will instead directly work with the JavaScript API. Before we begin, a small note of warning: even though the specification for this standard has not yet been finalized, most modern browsers support this feature quite well. Since the standard has changed during the past years, some older versions of current browsers may have slightly different implementations.

Let's have a look at how you create an audio element in JavaScript:

```
var audio = new Audio();
```

To find out what format the browser can play with JavaScript, you can use the canPlayType method. The basic usage would be:

```
var canPlay = audio.canPlayType('audio/ogg; codecs="vorbis"');
```

The problems begin with the possible values returned by this function: "probably", "maybe", "no", and "". This is probably far from what you would have expected, but there is a very good reason for this: depending on the format, it's not always possible for a decoder to know for sure if it's supported before accessing the file itself. Here is what those values mean:

- "probably": It's almost a yes! The browser knows the file type and is pretty sure it can decode almost all files of this type.

- "maybe": The browser knows the file format but also knows it doesn't support all variants of it. Another reason might be that the browser delegates the reading of this file to a plugin and has no way of being sure that the plugin can handle this particular file.

- "": The browser doesn't know about this file type and won't delegate the reading to a plugin either. With this response, you can safely assume that the file won't be played.

- "no": This is the same answer as ""; it was used by some early implementations of the standard. If you want to support older browsers too, you should expect this response sometime.

With this knowledge, what you would do to mimic the behavior of the HTML code we saw earlier is something like this:

```
var audio = new Audio();
var canPlayOggVorbis = audio.canPlayType('audio/ogg;
codecs="vorbis"');
```

```
var canPlayMP3 = audio.canPlayType('audio/mpeg; codecs="mp3"');
if (canPlayOggVorbis == "probably" || (canPlayOggVorbis == "maybe" &&
canPlayMP3 != "probably")) {
  sound.ext = ".ogg";
} else {
  sound.ext = ".mp3";
}
```

This has given the priority to Ogg Vorbis but gives the priority to `"probably"` over `"maybe"`, so if the browser can only *maybe* play Ogg Vorbis but thinks it can *probably* play MP3, we will load the MP3 version of the file.

Preloading a sound

In contrast to the `embed` tag, the `audio` element provides a way to manage the preloading of the sound. This is done through the `readyState` property of the `audio` element. It can have many possible values:

- `HAVE_NOTHING`: Either the file is not accessible or no data at all has been loaded until now; probably the former. The numerical value corresponding to this state is `0`.

- `HAVE_METADATA`: The very beginning of the file has been preloaded; this is enough to parse the metadata part of the sound. With that data, the duration of the sound can be parsed. The numerical value corresponding to this state is `1`.

- `HAVE_CURRENT_DATA`: The sound has been loaded up to the current playback position but not enough to continue playback. Most likely, this is due to the playback position being the end of the file since, usually, a state transition occurs very fast to the file below. The numerical value corresponding to this state is `2`.

- `HAVE_FUTURE_DATA`: The sound has been preloaded enough to start playing the rest of the file from the given playback position, but you have no guarantee that the playback won't stop soon to allow for more buffering. The numerical value corresponding to this state is `3`.

- `HAVE_ENOUGH_DATA`: Enough of the sound has been preloaded so that the sound should play entirely without interruption (this is an estimate based on the playback rate and download speed). The numerical value corresponding to this state is `4`.

For our implementation, we will consider a sound preloaded only if it's in the
HAVE_ENOUGH_DATA state. Let's have a look at the preloading implementation
of our small library:

```
// a sound object
sound = function(){

  // Preloads the sound
  this.preload = function(url){
    this.audio = new Audio();
    this.audio.preload = "auto";
    this.audio.src = url + sound.ext;
    this.audio.load();
  };

  // Returns true if the sound is preloaded
  this.isPreloaded = function(){
    return (this.audio.readyState == 4)
  }

  // ..
};

(function(){
  var audio = new Audio();
  var canPlayOggVorbis = audio.canPlayType('audio/ogg;
codecs="vorbis"');
  var canPlayMP3 = audio.canPlayType('audio/mpeg; codecs="mp3"');
  if (canPlayOggVorbis == "probably" || (canPlayOggVorbis == "maybe"
&& canPlayMP3 != "probably")) {
    sound.ext = ".ogg";
  } else {
    sound.ext = ".mp3";
  }
})();
```

There are two parts in the preceding code; we've already seen the highlighted
one—it's used to determine the supported sound format. It's wrapped in a function
that will be executed only once and stores the supported format in the sound object
as an object variable.

The rest of the code is the preloading implementation. First we create an `audio` object. Then we set the preloading mode to `auto`. This tells the browser that it can download as much as it wants from the file. After that, we point to the correct version of our file. Here you can see that the `src` argument is expected to omit the extension to allow the function to choose the correct version.

Finally, we call the `load` function. This is necessary for some implementations to actually start loading the file. We will consider the sound preloaded only for the value `HAVE_ENOUGH_DATA` of the `readyState` property.

Playing and stopping sounds

Controlling the playback is pretty easy. Let's first have a look at our implementation:

```
// Starts to play the sound. If loop is true the
// sound will repeat until stopped
this.play = function(loop){
  if (this.audio.lopp === undefined){
    this.audio.addEventListener('ended', function() {
        this.currentTime = 0;
        this.play();
    }, false);
  } else {
    this.audio.loop = loop;
  }
  this.audio.play();
};

// Stops the sound
this.stop = function(){
  this.audio.pause();
  this.audio.currentTime = 0;
};
```

The implantation of the `play` part is pretty straightforward. However, some older browsers don't support the `loop` attribute. For these, we need to loop manually. To achieve this, we register an event handler that will be called when the sound reaches its end. This event handler will simply rewind the sound and play it again.

As you can see, there is no `stop` function for the `audio` element, but there is a `pause` one. This means that if we call `start` again after a `pause` function, the sound will continue from where it was and will not start at the beginning. To rewind the sound, we set the current time to `0`, which means "at the beginning".

Having a `pause` function could be handy, so we will add one to our library:

```
// Pauses the sound
this.pause = function(loop){
  this.audio.pause();
};
```

Now you may think that this is a pretty good solution, and in most cases, it is. There are, however, a few problems with it; you cannot manipulate the sound much beyond changing its playback speed. Effects, panning (control of the repartition of the sound among the available output channels), and such are out of the question. Furthermore, on some devices (mostly mobile ones), you cannot play two sounds simultaneously. Most of the time, this is due to hardware limitations, but the result is that you cannot have background music and sound effects at the same time. If you want to use this API on iOS, you have to be aware that you can only start to play the sound in response to an event generated by the user.

Web Audio API

The Web Audio API aims to give the JavaScript developer basically the same tool he is used to having when writing a native application. It replicates the capabilities of OpenAL, a very widely used API for game development. Furthermore it's a standard API. Sadly, for the moment, it's only implemented on Webkit-based browsers including the mobile version in iOS 6.

Before work on this standard began, Mozilla added a similar API to Firefox called Audio Data and is currently working on migrating to the Web Audio API. It should probably be available in a stable version before the end of 2013. As for Internet Explorer, nothing has been announced yet. If you want to use the Web Audio API in Firefox, you can now use the `audionode.js` library (`https://github.com/corbanbrook/audionode.js`), but it's incomplete and hasn't been updated in years. However, if you stick to simple usage, it will probably do the trick!

Instead of simply providing a way to play a sound, this API provides a full stack to generate sound effects. This has the side effect of producing a slightly more complex API.

Basic usage

The idea behind the Web Audio API is that you connect nodes together in order to route a sound to the speakers. You can imagine those nodes as real-life devices such as amplifiers, equalizers, effect pedals, or CD players. All that is done in the Web Audio API is done through the Audio context. It's an instantiated object, but you can only have one instance of it at any given time.

Let's start with a very basic example by connecting an MP3 source to the speaker, as shown in the following figure:

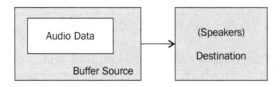

To create an MP3 source, you first need to load the sound. This is done through an asynchronous XML HTTP request. Once this is done, we have a file encoded as an MP3 that we will need to decode to obtain the bytes describing the sound wave and store them into a buffer:

```
var soundBuffer = null;
var context = new webkitAudioContext();

var request = new XMLHttpRequest();

request.open('GET', url, true);
request.responseType = 'arraybuffer';

// Decode asynchronously
request.onload = function() {
  context.decodeAudioData(request.response, function(buffer) {
    soundBuffer = buffer;
  }, onError);
}
request.send();

var context = new webkitAudioContext();
```

At this point, the `soundBuffer` object holds the decoded sound data. We then need to create a source node and connect it to the buffer. Metaphorically, this would be like putting a CD in the CD player:

```
var source = context.createBufferSource();
source.buffer = buffer;
```

Finally, we need to connect the source to the speakers:

```
source.connect(context.destination);
```

This is like connecting our CD player to a headset or some speakers. At this point, you won't hear anything because we still haven't played the sound. To do this, we can write the following:

```
source.start(0);
```

If the name of this method changed recently to make it more understandable, it used to be called `noteOn` so you may want to support this too, since the change is fairly recent and a few browsers may still have the old name implemented. If you want to stop playback, you will call `stop` (or its new name `noteOff`). You are probably wondering why we need to pass an argument to this function. That would be because this API allows you to synchronize audio in a very precise way to do whatever you want (another sound or a visual effect). The value you pass is the moment at which the sound should start to play (or stop). This value is given in seconds.

With what we've seen until now, we can already implement our small library, so let's do it before we have a look at the more complex usage:

```
sound = function(){
  this.preloaded = false;

  // Preloads the sound
  this.preload = function(url){
    var request = new XMLHttpRequest();
    request.open('GET', url, true);
    request.responseType = 'arraybuffer';

    // Decode asynchronously
    var that = this;
    request.onload = function() {
      sound.context.decodeAudioData(request.response, function(buffer)
{
        that.soundBuffer = buffer;
        that.preloaded = true;
      });
    }
    request.send();
  };

  // Returns true if the sound is preloaded
  this.isPreloaded = function(){
    return this.preloaded;
  }
```

```
// Starts to play the sound. If loop is true the
// sound will repeat until stopped
this.play = function(loop){
    this.source = sound.context.createBufferSource();
    this.source.buffer = this.soundBuffer;
    this.source.connect(sound.context.destination);
    this.source.loop = true;
    this.source.start(0);
};

// Stops the sound
this.stop = function(){
    this.source.stop(0);
};
};

sound.context = new webkitAudioContext();
```

There's nothing new here except that the `play` and `stop` functions can only be called once. This means that you have to create a new `bufferSource` object each time you want to play the sound.

Connecting more nodes

Let's add a new node to our context: a `gain` node. This node allows you to change the volume of your sound. The real-life version of this sound would be an amplifier. The following figure shows how our node will be connected:

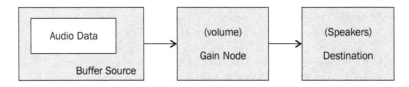

First let's create the node:

```
var gainNode = context.createGainNode();
```

Then we will connect our source to the node input and the speakers to the node output:

```
source.connect(gainNode);
gainNode.connect(context.destination);
```

Once this is done, we can modify the volume by changing the value of the `gain.value` property, as follows:

```
gainNode.gain.value = 0.8;
```

The `gain` parameter is something called `AudioParams`. It's a parameter you will find in a lot of nodes, and it possesses a series of functions that allow you to manipulate a value, not only immediately but also making it change over time.
Here are the functions you can call on this object:

- `setValueAtTime(value, time)`: This will change the value at the specified time. The time is the absolute time given in seconds, just as for the `start` function.

- `linearRampToValueAtTime(value, time)`: This will make the current value change linearly until it reaches the specified value at the provided time.

- `exponentialRampToValueAtTime(value, time)`: This will make the current value change exponentially until it reaches the specified value at the provided time.

- `setTargetAtTime(target, time, constant)`: This will make the current value approach the target value from the given time at a constant rate.

- `setValueCurveAtTime(valuesArray, time, duration)`: This will make the value go through all the values in the provided array from the provided time during the provided duration.

- `cancelScheduledValues(time)`: This will cancel all the programmed value changes from the given time.

The following figure shows examples of those functions:

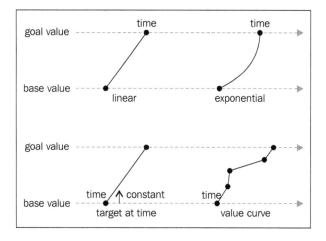

All these functions can be set up to chain one after the other. The exact way in which they will interact can sometimes be complex, and some transitions will create an error. For more details, you should have a look at the specs.

Loading more than one sound

This sound is just one among many available nodes you can use to create your sound graph. You can combine them as you want, and of course, connect more than one source to your `context.destination` object. If you want to use more than one sound, you will want to preload them all at once.

You could use the API we've seen to do this, but there is a way to do this out of the box in Web Audio by using `BufferLoader`. The following code shows how this works:

```
bufferLoader = new BufferLoader(
    context,
    [
        'sound1.mp3',
        'sound2.mp3'
    ],
    function(bufferList){
        // bufferList is an array of buffer
    }
);
bufferLoader.load();
```

The callback will be executed when the sound is buffered, just as with the `onload` callback in the previous example.

So many nodes, so little time

There is quite a number of effect nodes provided by this API; let's now have a quick overview of the nodes. This list is taken from the specifications (http://www.w3.org/TR/webaudio/). Keep in mind that the specifications are still evolving and the implementation is not always complete or up-to-date with the specifications.

Delay node

The **delay** node will simply delay the sounds coming in. It has only one parameter that represents the amount of time the sound should be delayed by.

ScriptProcessor node

This node is a general-purpose node that allows you to write your own effect in JavaScript. It has two parameters:

- `bufferSize`: This defines the size of the buffer, which has to be one of the following values: 256, 512, 1024, 2048, 4096, 8192, or 16384. The buffer is the part of the sound your JavaScript function will work on.

- `onaudioprocess`: This is the function that will modify your sound. It will receive an event as a parameter with the following properties: the node that called it, the input buffer, and the time at which the audio from the buffer will be played. The function will have to write the sound to the event's output buffer.

Panner node

This node will allow you to spatialize the sound in a 3D environment. You can define the sound source's spatial properties with the `setPosition`, `setOrientation`, and `setVelocity` functions. To modify the listener's spatial properties, you will have to access the `context.listener` object and use those same functions.

There are many mode parameters you can set on this node to fine-tune the ways the spatialization is done, but you'll have to look at the specs for the details.

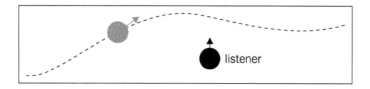

Convolver node

This node creates a **Convolver** effect (http://en.wikipedia.org/wiki/ Convolution). It takes two parameters: the buffer holding the sound wave used as an **impulse** for the convolution and a Boolean value that specifies whether the effect should be normalized or not.

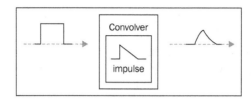

Analyser node

This node doesn't change the sound at all; instead, it can be used to do frequency and time-domain analyses.

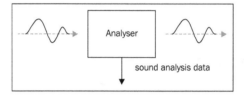

DynamicCompressor node

This node implements a compressor effect. You can configure the effect with the following parameters: **threshold**, **knee**, **ratio**, **reduction**, **attack**, and **release**.

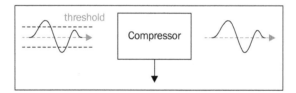

BiquadFilter node

This node can be used to apply a series of low-order filters. To specify which one you can use the node's `type` property to assign it one of the following values: `lowpass`, `highpass`, `bandpass`, `lowshelf`, `highshelf`, `peaking`, `notch`, and `allpass`. You can configure the chosen effect by setting some properties of the node. For details, you can have a look at the specs.

WaveShaper node

This node implements a waveshaper effect (http://en.wikipedia.org/wiki/Waveshaper) defined by its shaping function provided as an array in the curve properties of the node.

Flash fallbacks

This may seem strange, but there are a few situations where you may want to use Flash for sound. For example, you may have designed a simple game with HTML because you wanted to target iOS devices and desktops at the same time. But you want older browsers such as IE 6 to have sound too. Or you want to use only MP3 and provide Flash for devices that don't support it. Those are some situations where you may want to use Flash if the HTML5 Audio element is not supported.

There are some libraries that allow you to abstract this; we will take a detailed look at one of them—SoundManager 2—and then a quick overview of some available alternatives.

SoundManager 2

To use SoundManager 2 (http://www.schillmania.com/projects/soundmanager2/), you only need to include a smallish JavaScript code on your page and provide a link to the Flash files (hosted on the same server to comply with the same-origin policy). Let's have a quick look at what the implementation of preloading would look like.

```
sound = function(){

  this.preloadStarted = false;

  // Preloads the sound
  this.preload = function(url){
    if(sound.ready){
      this.audio = soundManager.createSound({
        id: 'sound'+sound.counter++,
        url: url,
        autoLoad: true,
        autoPlay: false,
        volume: 50
      });
      this.preloadStarted = true;
    } else {
```

```
      this.url = url;
    }
  };

  // Returns true if the sound is preloaded
  this.isPreloaded = function(){
    if (!this.preloadStarted){
      this.preload(this.url);
      return false;
    } else {
      return (this.audio.readyState == 3)
    }
  }
  //...
};

sound.ready = false;
sound.counter = 0;
// a sound object
soundManager.setup({
  url: 'sm2.swf',
  flashVersion: 8,
  useHTML5Audio: true,
  onready: function() {
    sound.ready = true;
  }
});
```

To use SoundManager 2, we first have to configure it; that's what the highlighted part of the preceding code does. The `url` parameter is the path to the Flash file that will be used to play the sound. We've chosen Flash Version 8 because you don't need a higher version if you want to mimic the HTML5 Audio element. We then set a flag to make the library use HTML5 to play the sound when Flash is not available. Since this method can take some time before all is loaded and ready to be used, we set an event handler to detect whether the `SoundManager` object is ready. This event handler simply sets a flag. There are more available parameters, and I recommend that you take a look at them in the well-written documentation for `SoundManager`.

To implement the `preload` function, we have to take into account that SoundManager may not be ready. If that is the case, we wait for the next call to `isPreloaded` to start the preloading (if `SoundManager` is ready at this point).

To query the status of the sound we can use the `readyState` parameter, but be careful; the available values are not the same as the ones for the HTML5 Audio element:

- `0`: Sound is not initialized; preloading has not started yet
- `1`: Sound is loading
- `2`: An error occurred during the loading of the sound
- `3`: The file has been loaded

Obviously, we will consider a sound as being ready if the `readyState` parameter has the value `3`. Here is the implementation of the last three methods; there is nothing special here since each of them has an exact match in `SoundManager`:

```
// Starts to play the sound. If loop is true the
// sound will repeat until stopped
this.play = function(loop){
  this.audio.loops = loop;
  this.audio.play();
};

// Pauses the sound
this.pause = function(loop){
  this.audio.pause();
};

// Stops the sound
this.stop = function(){
  this.audio.stop();
};
```

That's it for the SoundManager implementation of our sound library.

Alternatives to SoundManager

There are many other libraries that do what SoundManager does. jPlayer (`http://www.jplayer.org/`) is one of them. Contrary to what SoundManager does, it allows you to play video too and was conceived from the ground up around the HTML5 Audio and Video elements whereas this was added later to SoundManager. Furthermore, it's conceived as a jQuery plugin. However, it's conceived to be used as a media player, with a UI visible to the user. This can be disabled if you want to use it in your game.

Another possibility is that of using SoundJS (`http://www.createjs.com/#!/SoundJS`). It's a part of the CreateJS suite of tools and is well adapted to game programming. SoundJS supports HTML5 Audio, Web Audio API, and Flash. If you're familiar with CreateJS, using it should not be a problem; otherwise, it will probably seem a little harder to use than the two previous ones. I would argue that this is worth the effort since it's a very clean and modern library.

If you don't want to learn yet another library to play your sounds, you could use `mediaelement.js` (`http://mediaelementjs.com/`); it provides an implementation of the HTML5 Audio and Video elements for browsers that don't support it. If you use this library, you will simply write your code using the `audio` element, and a Flash or Silverlight script will be used to play it where needed.

Generating sound effects

Until now, we mostly spoke about music. Of course, the same techniques can be used to play sound effects. There is however a very elegant solution for dealing with them: generating them at runtime. This mimics the way a lot of effects were created on old game consoles. To do this in JavaScript, you can use `SFXR.js` (`https://github.com/humphd/sfxr.js`). It's a port of the popular SFXR. Sadly, it only works with Firefox's Audio Data API. Nevertheless, I would encourage you to check it out!

Summary

You have now learned lots of different ways to play sounds in your games using standard APIs, plugins, and Flash libraries, and your head is probably hurting right now! The state of audio in the browser is not very nice at the moment, but in a few years, when the Web Audio API is supported across all browsers, we will be in a much better situation! So, I would recommend spending some time on learning it well even if it's slightly more complex than the HTML5 Audio element.

You now have all the tools you need to create the perfect jQuery game! I really hope you enjoyed reading this book and that it will inspire you to create many wonderful games.

Index

Symbols

$.ajax function 97, 111
$.get 111
$.getJSON 111
$.getScript 111
$.load 111
$.post 111
.animate() function 10
.append() function 14
.bind() function 12
.clearQueue() function 11
.delay() function 11
.delegate() function 12, 13
.dequeue() function 11
.detach() function 15
.done() 115
.fail() 115
.html() function 14
.prepend() function 14
.remove() function 15
.stop() function 11

A

addCallback function 42
addSprite function 51
addTilemap function 86
analog joystick
  about 190
  event handlers 192, 193
  implementing 190, 191
Analyser node 218
animation function 76
animations
  adding, to framework 23, 24
chaining 10
implementing 22, 23
audio
  abstracting 202
audio, abstracting
  library, using 202, 203
audio element 208
audionode.js library 211
audio tag 206

B

BiquadFilter node 218
BrowserQuest
  URL 84

C

cancelScheduledValues(time) function 215
canPlayType method 207
chaining
  about 8
  advantages 8
cheating, preventing
  code, obfuscating 152, 153
  network protocol, making less readable 154
  server-side verification 149
  variables, making less readable 150, 151
colliding tiles
  searching 68, 69
collision detection
  about 35, 65, 94
  colliding tiles, finding 68, 69
  implementing 35-38
  player, versus environment collisions 94, 95
  player, versus sprite collision 97

jQuery Mobile
  URL 178
jQuery's API
  URL 16
JSON
  URL 125
JSON file
  loading 112, 113
jump method 76

K

keyboard polling, game optimization
  about 47
  keys state, tracking 48, 49

L

leaderboards
  about 143
  creating 144, 145
  highscores, displaying 148, 149
  highscores, retrieving 146, 148
  highscores, saving 145
Learning jQuery
  URL 16
library
  using 202, 203
linearRampToValueAtTime(value, time)
    function 215

M

main loop, game
  about 32
  implementing 33-35
mediaelement.js 222
MIDI 206
mobile browsers
  client-side browser detection 180, 181
  detecting 179
  feature detection, using 182
  server-side detection 181
mobile device
  capabilities 177

modulo technique 36
multi-file game
  $.ajax function, using 111
  call, debugging to $.ajax 114
  implementing 105, 106
  JSON file, loading 112, 113
  remote script, loading 113, 114
  sprites, loading 109-111
  tile map, loading 106-109
multiplayer game
  creating 121
  players account, managing 122
  server-side combat, implementing 138-141

N

naive implementation 64, 65
network traffic, protecting
  about 154
  random variables, adding 156, 157
  values, encoding 155
  variables, naming randomly 155
nodes
  connecting 214, 215, 216
NPCs
  implementing 99, 100

O

OAuth 158
object-oriented code, for player 72
offline application cache
  using 198, 199
offline divs 55, 56
OpenAL 211
optimizations, game
  HTML fragments 49-51
  intervals and timeouts, reducing 42
  keyboard polling 47
  one single interval, using 42, 43
  reflow, avoiding 51, 52
  requestAnimationFrame, using 53, 54
  sprite, animating using CSS Transforms 52, 53
orthogonal projection 83

P

Panner node 217
parallax scrolling 78
pause function 211
Pixen
  URL 21
platform game
  modifying 116-120
playback
  controlling 210, 211
player
  versus, environment collisions 94, 95
  versus, sprite collisions 97, 99
player control 77
players account, multiplayer game
  elements, searching in database 125, 126
  managing 122-124
  new player, creating in database 126-128
  player, keeping connected 129, 130
  user, logging into game 131
players avatar
  controlling 75, 76
players, keeping in sync
  about 131, 132
  client-side code 133-136
  current player position, updating 133
  players, retrieving 132, 133
players position
  updating 73-75
play function 205
polygonal collision detection 94
polymorphism
  about 8
  using 9
preload function 220
preloading 27, 28

Q

queues
  usage 11

R

readyState property 208
reflow
  avoiding 51, 52
remote script
  loading 113, 114
requestAnimationFrame
  using 53, 54
rgba() function 100

S

ScriptProcessor node
  about 217
  bufferSize parameter 217
  onaudioprocess parameter 217
server-side combat
  implementing, in multiplayer game 138-141
server-side helper library, Twitter API 161, 162
setInterval function 22, 42
setItem method 199
setOrientation function 217
setPosition function 217
setTargetAtTime(target, time, constant) function 215
setValueAtTime(value, time) function 215
setValueCurveAtTime(valuesArray, time, duration) function 215
setVelocity function 217
sound
  embedding 204
  preloading 208, 209
soundBuffer object 212
sound effects
  generating 222
sound, embedding
  implementation 204, 205
  supported formats 206
SoundJS 222
SoundManager
  alternatives 221, 222

SoundManager 2
  using 219-221
sounds
  playing 210, 211
  stopping 210, 211
sprite occlusion
  about 92
  managing 92
sprites
  about 21
  advantage 109
  advantages 21, 22
  animating 25-27
  animations, implementing 22, 23
  disadvantages 21, 110
sprite transformation
  about 59
  CSS transform 59, 60
startGame function 43
startPreloading function 30, 42
stop function 210
stop method 205

T

tile map editor
  using 95-97
tile map optimization
  about 84
  tile map, moving 87, 89
  visible tiles, finding 85, 86
tile maps
  about 62
  advantages 63, 107
  constraints 63
  loading 106
  naive implementation 64
top-down games
  tile map, moving 87-90
  tile map, optimizing 84, 85
  visible tiles, finding 85, 86
top-down perspective 83

touch control, mobile game
  about 185
  analog joystick 190, 191
  d-pad 186
touchend handler 193
touchstart event handler 192
Twitter 157
Twitter API
  about 158
  game, authenticating 162-164
  game, registering with Twitter 159-161
  highscores, publishing on Twitter 164-166
  logging in 159
  server-side helper library 161, 162
Twitter developer site
  URL 159
Twitter integration
  about 157
  Twitter API, accessing 158
  Twitter, for dummies 157, 158
twitteroauth library 161, 164

W

waitForSound function 203
WAV 206
WaveShaper node 219
Web Audio API
  about 211
  multiple sound, loading 216
  nodes, connecting 214-216
  usage 211-214
web storage
  using 199, 200
World of Ar'PiGi 122

Thank you for buying
jQuery Game Development Essentials

About Packt Publishing

Packt, pronounced 'packed', published its first book "*Mastering phpMyAdmin for Effective MySQL Management*" in April 2004 and subsequently continued to specialize in publishing highly focused books on specific technologies and solutions.

Our books and publications share the experiences of your fellow IT professionals in adapting and customizing today's systems, applications, and frameworks. Our solution based books give you the knowledge and power to customize the software and technologies you're using to get the job done. Packt books are more specific and less general than the IT books you have seen in the past. Our unique business model allows us to bring you more focused information, giving you more of what you need to know, and less of what you don't.

Packt is a modern, yet unique publishing company, which focuses on producing quality, cutting-edge books for communities of developers, administrators, and newbies alike. For more information, please visit our website: www.packtpub.com.

Writing for Packt

We welcome all inquiries from people who are interested in authoring. Book proposals should be sent to author@packtpub.com. If your book idea is still at an early stage and you would like to discuss it first before writing a formal book proposal, contact us; one of our commissioning editors will get in touch with you.

We're not just looking for published authors; if you have strong technical skills but no writing experience, our experienced editors can help you develop a writing career, or simply get some additional reward for your expertise.

Instant jQuery UI Starter

ISBN: 978-1-782168-23-2   Paperback: 36 pages

Discover how you can create rich end-user experiences for your web applications with jQuery UI

1. Learn something new in an Instant! A short, fast, focused guide delivering immediate results.

2. Learn how you can effectively utilize jQuery UI!

3. Refresh your JavaScript and jQuery skills

4. Quickly create Widgets and interactions

Instant Migration to HTML5 and CSS3 How-to

ISBN: 978-1-849695-74-9   Paperback: 68 pages

Discover how to upgrade your existing website to the latest HTML5 and CSS3 standards

1. Learn something new in an Instant! A short, fast, focused guide delivering immediate results.

2. Learn how to upgrade existing websites to HTML5 & CSS3 without changing appearance

3. Improve browser and mobile devices support for websites

4. Reduce the size of web pages by using the latest HTML5 elements and CSS3 features for faster, more-efficient websites

PUBLISHING

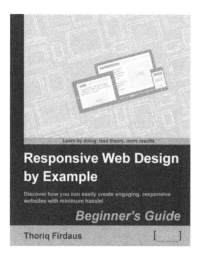

Responsive Web Design by Example

ISBN: 978-1-849695-42-8   Paperback: 338 pages

Discover how you can easily create engaging, responsive websites with minimum hassle!

1. Rapidly develop and prototype responsive websites by utilizing powerful open source frameworks

2. Focus less on the theory and more on results, with clear step-by-step instructions, previews, and examples to help you along the way

3. Learn how you can utilize three of the most powerful responsive frameworks available today: Bootstrap, Skeleton, and Zurb Foundation

Responsive Web Design with HTML5 and CSS3

ISBN: 978-1-849693-18-9   Paperback: 324 pages

Learn responsive design using HTML5 and CSS3 to adapt websites to any browser or screen size

1. Everything needed to code websites in HTML5 and CSS3 that are responsive to every device or screen size

2. Learn the main new features of HTML5 and use CSS3's stunning new capabilities including animations, transitions and transformations

3. Real world examples show how to progressively enhance a responsive design while providing fall backs for older browsers

Please check **www.PacktPub.com** for information on our titles

www.ingramcontent.com/pod-product-compliance
Lightning Source LLC
LaVergne TN
LVHW062313060326
832902LV00013B/2189